For all women,
past and living,
everywhere.

The Periodic Table Series

Periodically, we're all geeks about the things we love and the Periodic Table series has been created to celebrate this universal fact.

Inspired by The Periodic Table of Chemical Elements*, our experts have applied scientific logic to an eclectic range of subjects that regularly baffle beginners and fire-up fans. The outcome of this experiment is the essential guide you hold in your hands.

Geeky? Absolutely.
Hugely satisfying? Categorically.

*The Periodic Table of Chemical Elements orders all the known matter that makes up our world, from hydrogen to helium, by chemical properties and behavior to give scientists a handy overview of a rather complex subject.

To my mum and Ed—my two favorite feminists.

The Periodic Table of Feminism

by Marisa Bate

SEAL
PRESS

Seal Press
Hachette Book Group
1290 Avenue of the Americas, New York, NY 10104
sealpress.com
@SealPress

Printed in the United States of America

First published by Pop Press in 2018

First Seal Press edition: October 2018

Published by Seal Press, an imprint of Perseus Books, LLC, a subsidiary of Hachette
Book Group, Inc. The Seal Press name and logo is a trademark of the Hachette Book
Group.

The Hachette Speakers Bureau provides a wide range of authors for speaking events.
To find out more, go to www.hachettespeakersbureau.com or call (866) 376-6591.

The publisher is not responsible for websites (or their content) that are not owned by
the publisher.

Illustrations: Angeline Balayn

Original design: Seagull Design

Library of Congress Cataloging-in-Publication Data has been applied for.

ISBNs: 978-1-58005-868-1 (hardcover), 978-1-58005-869-8 (e-book)

Library of Congress Control Number: 2018954562

LSC-C

10 9 8 7 6 5 4 3 2 1

Contents

Introduction

The Periodic Table of Feminism

Feminism is a political, social and philosophical movement that has transformed and revolutionized women's lives. But feminism is also something else, something harder to articulate. It is a feeling in your gut, in your chest, in your eyes when they sting with hot tears or in your quivering voice in a moment of courage. Feminism is a drive, an energy, a constructive anger, an expression of hope for change, that keeps me, you, us, as it has done for millions of others, moving forward. It is a swell of a heart that is prepared to break for the greater good. Feminism is both a movement and something that can profoundly move us.

But *how* do you tell the story of feminism? Can you do justice to generations who have built and molded a movement? Can you capture the infinite ways by which women have lived and fought and struggled and won and lost? Can you truly convey where feminism sits in the great political, economic and social narratives of the last one hundred years or so? Ultimately, can you even have a Periodic Table of Feminism?

These are questions I have sincerely grappled with and this is the conclusion I have reached: this is *my* periodic table—one I want to share with as many readers as possible—but this is a periodic table that I built. It is categorically not the definitive periodic table of feminism. Because to truly understand feminism is to understand that it is not a singular narrative; it is not a dictatorship of behavior and opinions. Yes, there is a certain linear narrative: obtaining the vote; entering Parliament; legalizing abortion; legislating same-sex marriage. But these are facts that help pin down multiple threads of a movement as diverse and different as women. Feminism is a changeable, shape-shifting, transformative political endeavor to make women's lives better. That mission is the only constant—the method, the expression, the arrangement and the organization is multiple, often conflicting, always hopeful, never perfect.

At the start of this process I had one rule: the women in this book must have actively and deliberately chosen to help other women. There are plenty of women who are feminist icons because of what they have personally achieved and in turn how they inspire the next generation. But in the confines of this book, there had to be boundaries. The women you are about to meet had the *intention*, the *agenda* to promote, support and help other women—not by the proxy of personal achievement but as the root motivation of their actions.

After centuries of women's stories being intentionally forgotten or deemed unimportant, just shining a light on these women's lives is a feminist exercise in itself. But this table aims to situate those lives within the feminist movement, and also to paint a bigger picture of its place in the world.

Inside the movement, I wanted to track and trace how feminism's objectives transformed over time, from the fight for legal rights and personhood at the turn of the century to the demand for access to abortion, as well as the intellectualization of the movement in the 1960s and 1970s. I wanted to understand how, as Angela Davis has said, "the project of feminism" changed from issues of white women's liberation from domesticity and servitude to men to a focus on diversity. I wanted to appreciate how the same movement then gave birth to the anti-academic punk rock rage of Riot Grrrl and the rise of the hashtag warriors of the fourth wave. I wanted to show how, as much as the movement changed, some ideas became foundational. Simone de Beauvoir wrote, "One is not born but becomes a woman" in 1949. Her words would echo into the future and we find their relevance time and again across the table.

And what about outside the movement—the external forces that help change those internal discussions and shape feminism? Enlightenment thinking and the French Revolution prompted Mary Wollstonecraft to write what is considered the bible of western feminism. The suffragette movement was born out of an era of industrialization and rising belief in the rights of the under-classes. The political patchwork of the 20th century—fascism, communism, civil war—all played their part in sculpting the fight for women's rights.

So if you want to understand the political and social makeup of a nation, ask women about their lives. Choice, freedom and self-determination are often the stakes at play for women when political extremities take hold, and their presence or absence reveal a bigger story. Clara Campoamor helped write the Spanish Constitution in 1931, and in turn pushed through pioneering femi-nist legislation, before the arrival of Franco's dictatorship forced women's rights to regress. In the 1960s, Marxist factory strikes in northern Italy encouraged women to campaign for wages for housework—a movement that then spread across the world. At the same time, the civil rights movement burst through a dam that allowed the women's movements to follow—and as we witness racial hostility in America once again in recent times, we remember that three women created Black Lives Matter. I say this to make the point that the women's movement is not an isolated incident, as "women's issues" are often considered to be separate, unique only to women. No. Rather, they are the story of a whole society or a whole nation. They reflect who we all are. I wanted to show this movement—not only as the actions of brave individuals, but as a river flowing through the heart of history, being carried along by the determination of human endeavor, and carrying others along with it, too.

Of course, there is no way that all the women who deserve their story to be committed to paper could fit in this book. This book spans over 100 years and it would be like trying to fit a Tolstoyan epic into a single tweet. Instead, I hope the women I have chosen help to tell the story of many women like them. After all, we know that behind every great man there is a great woman, but what we should remember is that behind every great woman, there's at least a dozen more. When we do have the privilege of hearing a woman's voice we must listen, but we must also keep wondering whose voice aren't we hearing? In light of this I have tried to include the women who are already known heroes— but also introduce the lesser-known pioneers. Look out for the Dutch wonder woman Aletta Jacobs and then commit her name to memory. I have also endeavored to celebrate those fighting oppression and struggles on multiple fronts. As the electrifying Audre Lorde wrote, "I am not free while any woman is unfree, even when her shackles are very different from my own." It was Kimberlé Crenshaw in 1989 who finally gave a name to one of the few things feminism must be: intersectional.

Rebecca Solnit wrote, "Liberation is always in part a story-telling process; breaking stories, breaking silences, making new stories. A free person tells her own story. A valued person lives in a society in which her story has a place." Being able to tell the stories of these women is to give them the value they deserve— even if it's a value they never knew. We must know these stories because they are part of our stories, too—they inform us of where we've been and how we got where we are today. I hope these stories inspire and outrage and set something inside of you alight. I hope you will want to share them and they will propel you to tell your own—with all the courage and conviction and swollen hearts of these incredible women.

How the table works

So what's feminism got to do with the periodic table? Well, for starters, the language of chemistry lends itself readily to the lives of the women in the table; they are explosive free radicals, conductors and catalysts. They are reactionary, elemental, precious. They come together and create new, incredible things. If chemistry is the science of how things relate to one another and the world around them, then a feminist periodic table seems like a fine fit.

On the table itself, you will find like-minded individuals next to one another, grouped by the nature of their activism and their approach to the movement. Through the table you will see how women's ideas spoke to one another and connected with each other, across countries and across ideologies and across generations. From the table, you will see the ways in which the movement came together and pulled apart; and the way it was full of individuals who held very different beliefs, yet shared a common goal. The table is not a list of the "best" feminists, but the story of feminism. As Gloria Steinem has said of women and the fight for equality, "We are linked, not ranked."

The table is also categorized by waves. Caitlin Moran has said we're "post wave" and Julie Bindel once said, "there's enough waves in the sea, we don't need them in feminism," but it wouldn't be feminism if everyone was happy. The "waves" are just rough guidelines to help historically shape the periods we're talking about. Obviously, there aren't neat beginnings and endings—and plenty of women existed in between the ebbs and flows—but I hope they serve to show a broader sea change, not a precise science.

Finally, this table is just the beginning—it is the front of a march, the voices of those with the loudest megaphones. Follow these women to wherever they take you and then dare to go even further.

Proto-Feminists

1. **Bathsua Makin, 1600–1675**

   The middle-class Englishwoman was part of an emerging criticism of women's role in both society and at home. In 1673 she wrote, *An Essay to Revive the Ancient Education of Gentlewomen, in Religion, Manners, Arts & Tongues, with an Answer to the Objections against this Way of Education.*

2. **Christine de Pizan, 1364–1430**

   The medieval Italian-French author wrote poetry and prose as well as practical advice for women. In 1949, Simone de Beauvoir wrote that Pizan is "the first time we see a woman take up her pen in defence of her sex."

3. **Mary Astell, 1666–1731**

   Often described as the first English feminist, Astell was a writer who argued for equal education opportunities for women and that women were as rational as men. In 1694, she published *A Serious Proposal to the Ladies, for the Advancement of their True and Greatest Interest,* which included a plan for an all-female college.

4. **Aphra Behn, 1640–1689**

   The playwright, poet and fiction writer was one of the first women to earn a living writing. Virginia Woolf wrote of her, "All women together ought to let flowers fall upon the tomb of Aphra Behn...for it was she who earned them the right to speak their minds."

5. **Olympe de Gouges, 1748–1793**

   The revolutionary French feminist and abolitionist published *Declaration of the Rights of Woman and of the Female Citizen* in 1791. She argued for the equality of the sexes and she challenged male authority.

6. Toshiko Kishida, 1863–1901

One of Japan's first feminists, Kishida gave speeches including her most well-known, "Daughters in Box," which saw her arrested. Kishida argued that Japanese families were harming their daughters' freedom.

7. Bibi Khanoom Astarabadi, 1858–1921

Pioneering the Iranian women's movement, she founded the first school for girls in the modern history of the country. In 1895 she published *The Imperfections of Men*, considered by some as the first declaration of women's rights in the recent history of Iran.

8. Marie de Gournay, 1565–1645

"Happy are you, reader, if you do not belong to this sex to which all good is forbidden," wrote the French essayist in 1622 in her proto-feminist work *The Equality of Men and Women*.

9. Ching Shih, 1775–1844

A Chinese feminist pirate lord, she rose from prostitute to commanding 80,000 outlaws. Under her rule, rape was punishable by death.

10. Queen Nzinga, 1583–1663

The fearless African queen was the ruler of modern-day Angola and a shrewd international power player.

The
First
Wave

"Votes for women!"

This was the First Wave's rallying cry against a backdrop of modernizing industrialization, the spread of liberal ideas and mounting challenges to political and social order.

While we are right to think of the First Wave through a purple, white and green haze, the fight for suffrage was the pinnacle of a wider struggle for personhood; for ownership of women's own lives and identities; for their voices, ambitions, needs and ideas to be heard and acknowledged.

In this chapter you will meet a generation of "firsts": radicals, pioneers and visionaries who bravely reimagined what a woman's life could look like, and did whatever they could to make it a reality.

You will meet women who fought to take legal possession of not only themselves but of their children and money.

You will meet women who fought for access into the realms from which they had been excluded: the worlds of science, law, medicine, government and journalism.

You will meet women who fought to make the lives of their working sisters better, demanding eight-hour days, free education and childcare.

You will meet women who dedicated their lives to making birth control readily available to any who wanted or needed it.

You will meet African-American women, some born into slavery, who understood the intersectional nature of their oppression and articulated it over a century before Kimberlé Crenshaw coined the term.

And, from meeting these women, you will understand how the tectonic plates of the world shifted from one century to another. From falling monarchs to rising empires, from unification to the growth of fascism and socialism, the world changed and the fight for women's rights shifted with it.

The women you will meet here are only the tip of a feminist iceberg that began to dislodge patriarchal convention and oppression. History has a nasty habit of forgetting brilliant women, and yet the following pages cannot pay tribute to every single woman who fought to change the world. These are just a few of them, the ones whose stories tell the narratives that shaped this period. The women included here will make your heart race with their dedication, their fight, their relentless vision and their refusal to give in.

MARY WOLLSTONECRAFT

Visionary philosopher, writer and teacher
UK; 1759–1797

The "mother of feminism" Mary Wollstonecraft wrote one of the founding western feminist texts, *A Vindication of the Rights of Woman*, in 1792.

A passionate call to arms, the short pamphlet demanded women reject the oppressive conventions of society, based on superficial ideas of beauty and femininity, and educate themselves to independence with reason and intellect, traits they had been wrongly told belonged to men, and men only.

It could be argued that the seeds of Wollestonecraft's feminism were sown in her childhood. As a girl, Wollestonecraft often slept in front of her mother's door to protect her from her drunk, violent father. She was outraged by the fact her brother spent more time at school than she did, and that he would inherit more. These personal experiences, along with the Enlightenment thinking she was exposed to throughout her life, led Wollstonecraft to believe that only education could keep women safe from the pitfalls and prejudices of men.

So, aged 25, Wollstonecraft set up a school for girls with her sister. During this time, she also made friends with key thinkers of the day, including Thomas Jefferson and Benjamin Franklin, no less. Wollstonecraft began to publish her writings later in life, including *A Vindication of the Rights of Men*, a riposte to Edmund Burke's damning take on the French Revolution, followed by *A Vindication of the Rights of Woman*, which Virginia Woolf famously wrote inspired new "experiments in living."

Over 100 years after it was written, this text was used to propel the suffragette movement and it is still published around the world to this day.

the beginning
is always
today

Mary Wollstonecraft

EMMELINE PANKHURST

Passionate and radical suffragette
UK; 1858–1928

Emmeline Pankhurst was the leader of the British Suffragette movement.

Born in a Manchester suburb to political parents, she founded the Women's Social and Political Union (WSPU) in 1903, a nonpartisan group that included women of all classes and ages in the struggle for the vote.

The WSPU was born from Pankhurst's frustration. She could see little progress being made by the constitutional approach of the Suffragists. Instead, Pankhurst believed radical action was needed. Along with her three daughters, Christabel, Sylvia and Adela, the WSPU decided that they would do whatever it took to achieve votes for women.

They insisted on "deeds not words," a belief which led them to civil disobedience and vandalism, such as throwing stones through windows and setting alight letterboxes. Pankhurst once said "the argument of the broken window pane is the most valuable argument in politics."

After numerous arrests, hunger strikes, force-feeding and Christabel Pankhurst fleeing the country, the movement dispersed on the eve of the First World War. Tragically, Emmeline Pankhurst died on June 14, 1928, just weeks before the Equal Franchise Act was passed on the July 2, which gave the vote to all women over 21.

The lengths Emmeline Pankhurst went to to reach equality have rightfully earned her a place in history, and in 1999, on the eve of the millennium, *Time* magazine named Pankhurst "one of the most important people of the 20th century." Pankhurst inspired countless women when she was alive, triggering the fight for the vote around the world, and she continues to inspire 89 years later, with an urgency that feels relevant today.

i would rather
be a rebel
than a slave

Emmeline Pankhurst

EMILY WILDING DAVISON

Daring political prisoner
UK; 1872–1913

Emily Wilding Davison's death—killed as she ran in front of the King's horse in 1913—has become the ultimate symbol of Suffragette sacrifice.

However, long before that moment, Davison displayed her commitment to the Suffragette cause. She was arrested nine times and force-fed 49 times while in prison—a tactic that became synonymous with the militant suffragette movement.

On the night of the April 2, 1911, Davison hid in a cupboard in the Palace of Westminster during the census in order to claim the House of Commons as her residence on her census form and protest the political exclusion of women from voting and from Parliament itself. Today, thanks to the late Labour MP Tony Benn, the cupboard bears a plaque and picture to remember her.

Two years on from this census, on June 4, 1913, Davison was trampled to death by the King's horse at the Epsom races. For decades, it was unclear whether her death was accidental—a stunt gone wrong, or political martyrdom? (A return train ticket was found on her person.)

In 2013, new technology was able to reexamine the footage from the three surviving newsreels of the race, revealing that Davison had actually been trying to tie a scarf of the Suffragette colors to the King's horse. It was a tragic accident.

Her death was not in vain; her act has become the ultimate symbol of Suffragette sacrifice.

HENRIETTA DUGDALE

Relentless fighter
Australia; 1827–1918

Henrietta Dugdale was a tireless fighter for women's rights, helping to make Australia the second country in the world to grant women the right to vote in 1902.

In 1884, Dugdale formed the first Women's Suffrage group in Victoria. However, her campaign really began back in 1869 when she wrote to a local newspaper about the Married Women's Property Bill: "Some there are who say, 'If we permit woman to go beyond her sphere, domestic duties will be neglected.' In plainer language, 'If we acknowledge woman is human, we shall not get so much work out of her.'"

Alongside this, Dugdale campaigned for women's dress reform, access to university and education for the working classes. She also called for the eight-hour working day. By 1886, Dugdale's suffrage group had over 300 members. She was 75 when Australia gave women the vote.

While this was a triumph for Women's Suffrage in Australia, it's important to note that it wasn't until 1962 that Aboriginal men and women were given voting rights.

VIDA GOLDSTEIN

Parliamentarian
Australia; 1869–1949

Vida Goldstein was the first woman in the British Empire to stand for election to a national parliament.

Her first foray into politics came when she helped her mother, an Australian Suffragist, collect signatures for the so-called "Monster Petition" in 1891 calling for women's suffrage. Although it failed initially, it sparked Goldstein's interest in the movement. As a result, Goldstein turned down offers of marriage to dedicate her life to the cause. She became one of the leaders of the movement, got involved with workers' rights via the Anti-Sweating League, founded a newspaper called *The Woman Voter*, and went to the first international suffrage conference in Washington DC in 1902, where, according to one historian, she was treated like a rock star on arrival.

One of the reasons for the reception was presumably because Australia had just become the first country in the world to give women both the right to vote in federal elections and also the right to be elected to Parliament on a national basis.

This was Goldstein's chance and although she was never elected, she ran for Parliament four times in total.

"Nothing was more degrading than for a woman to have to marry for a home. Love should be the sole reason. Surely those with a brain to think, eyes to see and mind to reason must realize that the capitalist system must cease and a cooperative system prevail in its place?"

Vida Goldstein

KATE SHEPPARD

First victor in the fight for the vote
New Zealand; 1847–1934

Kate Sheppard led the first victory in the world for a woman's right to vote.

In 1883, New Zealand became the first country in the world to introduce universal suffrage and leading that movement was Liverpool-born Kate Sheppard. Sheppard's fight for Suffrage was born from her involvement with the Temperance movement—the Christian campaign to limit the sale of alcohol—and, in 1885, Sheppard helped found the Women's Christian Temperance movement in New Zealand, and went about lobbying for the women's vote in order to further an anti-liquor agenda.

Soon, however, for Sheppard the fight for suffrage became a goal in itself.

In 1893, Sheppard presented the largest ever petition of the time to Parliament with 32,000 signatures. Both Parliaments passed the Act and universal suffrage became law on September 19 that year.

After her success in New Zealand, Sheppard travelled all over the world helping to support the suffrage movement. Today she appears on the New Zealand $10 note—the only woman to do so.

THE FAMOUS FIVE

Stronger united
Canada

"Does the word 'Persons' in Section 24 of the British North America Act, 1867, include female persons?"

This was the question that united five Canadian feminists to challenge the law that prohibited women from the senate. When they were told that "Persons" did not include women, they mounted a challenge that went all the way to Canada's highest court—and won.

we are tired of
having a sphere
doled out to us, and of
being told that
anything outside
that sphere is
'unwomanly'

Kate Sheppard

"Never explain,
never retract,
never apologize.
Just get the thing
done and let them
howl."

Nellie McClung of The Famous Five

The Famous Five were led by Emily Murphy and included Nellie McClung, Henrietta Muir Edwards, Irene Parlby and Louise McKinney.

All of these women were impressive in their own right.

Emily Murphy became the first female magistrate in the British Empire in 1916. She had also been pivotal in creating the Married Women's Property Act in 1870, which gave women greater property rights. Henrietta Edwards helped found the National Council for Women in 1895. Louise McKinney was the first woman elected to sit as a Member of the Legislative Assembly in the British Empire and Irene Parlby was an advocate of farm women in Western Canada. The efforts of Nellie McClung saw Manitoba become the first province to let women not only cast a ballot but also run for office.

ALETTA JACOBS

Visionary medic
The Netherlands; 1854–1929

"You should have her doing the washing instead of packing her off to a university with a pile of books under her arm." These are the words of Aletta Jacobs' disgruntled brother. When Jacobs demanded access to higher education, he clearly disagreed.

Nevertheless, she persisted.

Jacobs was a visionary, a pioneer and a tireless supporter of women. She was the first woman to study at university level and to receive a medical doctorate in the Netherlands.

After Jacobs graduated in 1879, she took a short trip to London where she encountered radical thinkers promoting suffrage and birth control. On returning to Amsterdam, she opened a practice in the poorer district of the city in 1880. Here she encountered the plight of the working classes, becoming aware of the effects of multiple births on a woman's body and the impact of impoverishment. As part of her practice, Jacobs set up what is believed to be the first birth-control clinic in the world. For 14 years, two mornings a week, she provided free advice and contraception for women, including prostitutes.

Alongside this, Jacobs led the Dutch suffrage movement, and campaigned to decriminalize prostitution and protect women workers' rights. She was also an outspoken pacifist.

MARIA TERESA FERRARI

Educator
Argentina; 1887–1956

In 1939, María Teresa Ferrari became the first female university professor in the whole of Latin America and she used her unique status to further research to revolutionize women's healthcare in both Argentina and Brazil.

After time spent studying medicine in America and Europe, Ferrari brought back methods to Argentina, setting up a maternity ward and introducing gynacological services at the military hospital. She also pioneered treatments, including radiation use for uterine tumors and development of a vaginoscope. Not only did Ferrari's own actions help push forward the women's movement in Argentina, but she was keen to empower others. In 1936, she established the Argentine Federation of University Women to help create a pipeline for greater female representation in Argentine society.

ELIZABETH GARRETT ANDERSON

Pioneering British surgeon
UK; 1836–1917

Elizabeth Garrett Anderson was a pioneering woman of firsts.

She was the first woman to qualify as a surgeon in Britain, the first female dean of a medical school, the first female member of the British Medical Association, the first female mayor, and co-founded the first hospital to be staffed by women.

Inspired by those she met in her youth, such as feminist Emily Davies and physician Elizabeth Blackwell, Anderson had a trailblazing medical career fuelled by a deliberate feminist commitment.

She opened her own practice offering help to poor women, followed by a dispensary that eventually became the New Hospital for Women and Children in 1872. In 1874, she co-founded the London School of Medicine for Women—the only teaching school in the country to admit women.

In honor of her lifelong determination to both aid and socially advance women, in 1918, the New Hospital was given her name and today, a secondary school in Islington is also named after her.

18   1
Ms
Margaret
Sanger

MARGARET SANGER

Crusader for access to birth control
USA; 1879–1966

Margaret Sanger did not relent.

Her mother was pregnant 18 times, with 11 babies born alive and seven stillborn, and died aged 50 from the stress of constant pregnancy. Watching her mother—and working as a nurse with poor immigrant families in New York at the turn of the century—Sanger was determined to prevent more women facing a similar fate.

She was visionary and radical, popularizing the term "birth control" in 1910. Under the 1873 Comstock Act, it was illegal to distribute or promote contraception, but this didn't stop her. In 1914, Sanger was indicted and fled to the UK after publishing The Woman Rebel, a radical eight-page pro-birth-control monthly newsletter.

Sanger returned to New York and opened the first family-planning clinic in America on October 16, 1916. An undercover police officer was one of the clinic's first visitors. She was arrested and sentenced to 30 days in the workhouse.

After the war, Sanger set up the American Birth Control League—the foundation of today's Planned Parenthood. By 1937, in large part thanks to her actions, contraception was deemed standard practice for doctors to prescribe.

Her final act was to be instrumental in encouraging the philanthropist Katharine McCormick to fund the development of the first contraceptive pill—the gateway to the sexual revolution and the women's liberation movement.

Sanger's lifelong commitment to giving women access to safe birth control tells the story of women in the 20th century: the battle for freedom, social mobility, for control over their own bodies and sexuality.

JOSEPHINE BUTLER

Tireless campaigner
UK; 1828–1906

Called "Britain's first anti-prostitution campaigner," "one of our greatest social reformers" and "one of the bravest and most imaginative feminists in history," Josephine Butler's achievements are staggering.

She campaigned tirelessly against prostitution and slavery and worked for the rights of "fallen women"—a passion that accelerated after the death of her infant daughter when it became her sole focus. Through her campaigning, the Contagious Diseases Act, first passed in 1864, which saw prostitutes arrested and imprisoned for carrying sexually transmitted diseases often given to them by British military, was repealed in 1886, and Butler took the campaign to India and parts of Europe.

She worked with women in workhouses and women who were sold into sex trafficking, organizing an international association to lobby against the practice, and set up her own sanctuary for prostitutes. Later on in life, she turned her attention to child prostitution and was key in raising the legal age of consent from 12 to 16.

As governments are still shaping the legislation around prostitutes today, and as contemporary sex workers demand their own rights, Butler's work can be criticized for its religious motivations and what some consider her patronizing ideas toward women's choices. Yet what is unquestionable is Butler's commitment to vulnerable women, trying to emancipate women and girls from sexual abuse and exploitation by the powerful men around them.

72   1

Mft

Millicent
Fawcett

MILLICENT FAWCETT

Political protester
UK; 1847–1929

It was Elizabeth Garrett Anderson, Millicent Fawcett's big sister, and Emily Davies who put the idea of suffrage into Millicent Fawcett's head. "We must see about getting the vote" Davies said to the sisters. "You are younger than we are, Millie, so you must attend to that." And that's precisely what she did.

These early ideas were then cemented by a speech Fawcett heard given by radical MP John Stuart Mill in 1865 and, at the age of just 19, Fawcett created the first ever parliamentary petition for women's suffrage.

And so began a lifetime commitment to achieving suffrage. Fawcett's methods were peaceful and constitutional—lobbying MPs, writing letters and creating petitions—in contrast to the disruptive "deeds" of the Suffragettes. For this reason, Fawcett and her supporters were known as Suffragists.

By the 1890s, there were 17 groups advocating suffrage and eventually they came under one umbrella, led by Fawcett, as the National Union of Suffrage Societies. The organization continued to lobby the Liberal Party, believing that was the fastest route to the vote. However, many historians have questioned the overly-hopeful trust Fawcett placed in the Liberal MPs of that time.

Instead, it's widely believed that it was the war that forced the British government to eventually relent. In 1918, the Representation of the People Act was passed that allowed married women or women with property over the age of 30 to vote. It wasn't for another decade, in 1928, that the vote was granted to all women and men over 21 with the Equal Franchise Act. Millicent Fawcett died the following year.

In 2016, J K Rowling, Emma Watson and Caroline Criado Perez sent a petition to the Mayor of London successfully calling for a statue of Fawcett in Parliament Square. The statue will be put up in 2018, to mark 100 years since British women were given the vote.

17 1
Mf
Margaret
Fuller

MARGARET FULLER

Fiery poet
USA; 1810–1850

"Humanity," said Edgar Allan Poe, "is divided into men, women and Margaret Fuller."

Like many threatened men, Poe's words were intended to be cruel but instead reflect how Fuller, as journalist, writer and poet, unapologetically defied the expectations of her time, rallying against convention, both in her ideas and in her actions.

Fuller showed a fierce intellect from a very young age, schooled by her Harvard-educated father. After his death, she became a teacher to provide for her family and also gave lectures to all-female audiences.

In 1839 Fuller became editor of *The Dial*, the transcendentalist movement's magazine, appointed by Ralph Waldo Emerson, with whom she famously had an intense relationship (although ambiguous in its exact nature).

It was in *The Dial* in 1843 that Fuller published "The Great Lawsuit. Man versus Men. Woman versus Women." Two years later it was expanded and published as *Woman in the Nineteenth Century.*

The feminist manifesto sold out in a week and has since been considered America's first feminist text, likening women to slaves in the minds of men. After publication, she became America's first female member of the press and first female war correspondent.

Sadly, Fuller's radical mind, career and ambition were too much for many men of her time. Yet Fuller's spirit could not be dampened. "I am 'too fiery'" … she wrote, "Yet I think to be seen as I am, and would lose all rather than softer anything away."

43   1

St

Sojourner
Truth

SOJOURNER TRUTH

Speaker of truth
American; c. 1797–1883

"And ain't I a woman? I could work as much and eat as much as a man—when I could get it—and bear the lash as well! And ain't I a woman? I have borne thirteen children, and seen most all sold off to slavery, and when I cried out with my mother's grief, none but Jesus heard me! And ain't I a woman?"

This was part of Sojourner Truth's speech at the Women's Convention in Ohio in 1851, which became emblematic of black women's struggle, quoted throughout the Civil War, and through history since. Over a hundred years after that speech, in 1981, influential second wave feminist bell hooks published *Ain't I a Woman? Black Women and Feminism*.

Isabella ("Belle") Baumfree changed her name after claiming she had a vision from God and became a preacher called Sojourner Truth. Born into slavery, repeatedly sold off and beaten, Truth eventually escaped with her young daughter in 1826. On trying to free her other children after the Emancipation Act of 1827, she found her son had been illegally sold off. She took the slave owner to court, sued him and won. She was the first black woman to do so.

Truth gave rousing lectures on abolition and women's suffrage and moral reform. She collected clothing for black regiments during the Civil War and afterward immersed herself in supporting freed people.

Truth became the first black woman honored with a bust in the U.S. Capitol and in 2016 it was announced she would appear on the U.S. $10 bill.

truth is powerful
and it prevails

Sojourner Truth

46   1
Fh
Frances
Harper

FRANCES HARPER

Abolitionist poet
USA; 1825–1911

Frances Harper was a fierce intellectual: an author, poet, abolitionist-lecturer and one of the first black novelists.

When, in 1893, Harper gave a speech at the World's Columbian Exhibition in Chicago, during the World's Congress of Representative Women, she told the audience she felt that they were standing on the "threshold of the women's era."

A few years later, in the face of the heinous Jim Crow laws, she helped found the National Association of Colored Women, along with Harriet Tubman, which was followed by the First National Conference of the Colored Women of America. Shortly after, in 1896, the National Federation of Colored Women and National League of Colored Women united in Washington. As Yale professor Hazel V Carby has written, "For the first time, black women were nationally organized to confront the various modes of their oppression."

The many forms of oppression that black women faced were explored in Harper's fiction, poetry and the rousing speeches and lectures she gave. She was widely praised for her brilliant oratory, and often confronted white-only female audiences with her messages.

She strove to define how a fairer society could be created for all, believing that enfranchised women would play a crucial role in this.

IDA B WELLS

Radical voice of truth
USA; 1862–1931

Ida B Wells has been called the "loudest and most persistent voice for truth" of her time.

Born into slavery in Mississippi during the Civil War, then orphaned as a teenager, Wells went on to teach to provide for her siblings before becoming an investigative journalist.

Wells used her journalism, a passion she believed to be the greatest weapon against discrimination, to campaign against lynching. She also became a prominent voice to defend black men against the white perception of their supposed lustful threat to white women—a viewpoint that saw her exiled to the north.

Academics have since praised Wells for the sophistication of her analysis, understanding how the structures of gender and racial oppression are interwoven. Wells suggested that allowing white men to protect the honor of white women was an act of oppression, both permitting the murder of black men and projecting onto black men their own history of sexual violence against women.

Wells' radical approach was a feature throughout her life. In 1883, she sat in the first class women's carriage of a train only to be told to move to second class because she was black. Wells bit the conductor and took the train company to court. On December 24, 1884, she won the case.

She challenged conventional gender norms of the time by owning her own newspaper, *The Memphis Free Speech,* refusing to relinquish her name when she married and operating with an unapologetic militancy that saw her postpone her own wedding three times.

the way to right
wrongs is to turn
the light of truth
upon them

Ida B Wells

66   1

Sa

Stanton/
Anthony

ELIZABETH CADY STANTON AND SUSAN B ANTHONY

America's founding mothers
USA; 1815–1902, 1820–1906

You can't read about one of these women without the other's name being mentioned in the same sentence, and their friendship drove the fight for the enfranchisement of women in America.

Susan B Anthony, who was raised in a Quaker family that promoted equality and was involved in the abolitionist movement, eventually became known as "the Napoleon of the women's movement."

Elizabeth Cady Stanton, who had received an excellent education after her only brother died, organized what is believed to be the world's first women's rights convention in Seneca Falls in 1848 and was active in creating the Married Women's Property Act, which granted women the right to own property, engage in business, manage their wages and be joint guardian of their children. Stanton married abolitionist Henry B. Stanton and together they had seven children.

In 1851, Stanton and Anthony met at an anti-slavery convention and a lifelong commitment to women's suffrage began. Their achievements include founding the Women's State Temperance Society (after Anthony was prevented from speaking at a conference because she was female), founding the Women's Loyal National League in support of the abolition of slavery, initiating the American Equal Rights Association (which campaigned for equal rights for both women and African-Americans) and founding the National Woman Suffrage Association. They also founded and edited a feminist newspaper, *The Revolution*.

In 1872, Anthony was arrested and convicted for voting, however, she refused to pay the fine, and the authorities dropped further action. Six years later, in 1878, Anthony and Stanton arranged for Congress to be presented with an amendment giving women the right to vote, which would become known as the Anthony Amendment. It passed and became the Nineteenth Amendment to the U.S. Constitution in 1920.

men, their rights and
nothing more;
women, their rights and
nothing less

Susan B Anthony

However, the story of Anthony and Stanton is not the feminist fairy tale it might seem. Despite their early work to enfranchise black men and women, the pair have been accused of ignoring the plight of black suffrage and colluding with white supremacists to further their cause (pro-slavery businessman George Train funded their newspaper). Most significantly, in 1869, they opposed the 15th Amendment which sought to allow black men to vote, but not women. Famously, Anthony said "I will cut off this right arm of mine before I will ever work or demand the ballot for the Negro and not the woman." More widely, the American suffrage movement, particularly in the south, has been accused of racism, excluding black women and even condoning lynching.

EMMA GOLDMAN

Dangerous anarchist
Russian Jewish immigrant, USA; 1869–1940

J Edgar Hoover of the FBI called Emma Goldman "one of the most dangerous women in America." United States Attorney Francis Caffey called her an "exceedingly dangerous woman."

Emma Goldman was an anarchist. Her ideas spread like wildfire; as a skilled and powerful orator she'd draw crowds of thousands. And she was "dangerous"—she was arrested for distributing information about contraception, was involved in the assassination attempt of a prominent industrialist, and was a firm believer in "the propaganda of the deed"—the anarchist belief that action can spark revolution.

But it was her ideas that the establishment was most afraid of. "There is nothing wrong with Emma Goldman," said the editor of the St. Louis *Mirror* newspaper in 1908, "except that she is 800 years ahead of her time."

She was one of the first Americans to openly support gay relationships, an atheist and, after her own experience as a working-class refugee, she called for radical workers' rights.

Goldman rejected the efforts of the suffragettes, believing that they did not challenge the link between state and economic power within a woman's oppression. Instead, Goldman has been

if i can't dance to it,
it's not my revolution

Emma Goldman

credited with creating anarcha-feminism, demanding a liberation from the patriarchy and its manifestation through capitalism and class struggle.

Her approach to the rights of women was as pioneering as the rest of her ideology.

ALEXANDRA KOLLONTAI

Forward thinker
Russia; 1872–1952

Alexandra Kollontai was arguably the most prominent woman in Lenin's government and is described by her biographer as "one of the most famous women in Russian history."

A young woman on the eve of the Russian Revolution, Kollontai was reading popular and Marxist literature, as well as occasionally working at a library that promoted socialist ideas and literacy lessons to workers. After leaving her husband and children and spending a brief time abroad, where she met Lenin, she returned to Russia and at age 27 joined the Russian Social Democratic Party, at first siding with the Mensheviks' faction before becoming a Bolshevik.

After the Bolshevik revolution of 1917, Kollontai was appointed People's Commissar for Social Welfare. She was the most prominent woman in the Soviet administration, and in 1919, she introduced the women's department.

Kollontai used her tremendous influence in a feminist way even though she rejected "feminism" as the indulgence of the liberal bourgeoisie. Under her leadership, married women were granted more rights, abortion was legalized, homosexuality was legalized and free public childcare was set up for working women. She believed in free love and rejected the patriarchal notion of marriage and traditional family life.

Throughout her time in the government, however, Kollontai faced resistance—in part for her open criticism of the Communist Party and her membership in the Workers' Opposition (she was the only member to survive the fatal "purges") but also for her alleged "feminist deviation." Essentially exiled, she was USSR diplomat for Mexico and Norway before settling in Sweden, becoming the first Western female diplomat, and she is credited for Sweden's decision to remain neutral during the Second World War.

ANNA FILOSOFOVA

Radical philanthropist
Russia; 1837–1912

Philanthropist Anna Pavlovna Filosofova is considered one of the leaders of Russia's first generation of feminists.

Influenced by her tyrannical father-in-law's treatment of his workers, Filosofova and her friend Maria Trubnikova set up a "Society for Cheap Lodging and Other Aid to the Residents of Saint Petersburg"—a place for homeless and battered women. These residences included a school, dormitories, a childcare center, cafeteria and a shop. Filosofova also set up the Society for the Organization of Women Who Work and a publishing house run entirely by women, putting into practice her strong belief in creating self-sufficiency. After the revolution of 1905, Filosofova joined the newly-permitted women's rights movement.

She also furiously lobbied the Czar to allow higher education for women. Through her campaigning, she was influential in the government approving Bestuzhev courses (higher-education courses for women). Filosofova became more radical as she became older, allegedly helping exiled revolutionaries flee Russia. As academic Rochelle Goldberg Ruthchild has written, "She remained an engaged and feisty feminist until her death."

SOPHIE ADLERSPARRE

Founding feminist
Sweden; 1823–1895

Sophie Adlersparre dedicated her life to encouraging independence, education and equality.

In 1859, Adlersparre, along with Rosalie Roos, launched Home
Review, the first Scandinavian women's magazine, credited with
kickstarting the feminist movement in Sweden, and providing a
unique space to discuss women's rights.

From here, Adlersparre organized educational evening classes
and a secretarial bureau to promote self-sufficiency. She peti-
tioned Parliament to allow women to study at the Royal Academy
of Art on equal terms as men, to aid budding female artists. In
1866, she co-founded the Stockholm Reading Parlour, a free
library for women, thereby giving all women access to the greatest
tool: books. She also co-founded Friends of Handicraft, in 1874,
as a sort of union to protect what was an important source of
income for women.

Adlersparre also set up Sweden's first feminist organization, the Fredrika Bremer Association, in 1884, which still exists
today. Fredrika Bremer (1801–1865) was an author who is often
likened to Jane Austen and wrote the seminal novel *Hertha* in
1856. This was a feminist victory in itself as it prompted a social
movement that granted Swedish women legal majority at the age
of 25. Adlersparre was hugely inspired by Bremer and wrote an
extensive autobiography of her, with the help of her niece.

The Fredrika Bremer Association sought to encourage
women in public life, informing them of their rights and how to
exercise them, and preparing them to serve on public boards.
Adlersparre led by example: in 1885, she became one of the first
two women to be a member of the state committee in Sweden.
Years later, after Adlersparre's death, the association became a
key vehicle in the push for suffrage.

women need work
and work needs
women

Sophie Adlersparre

MARIE STRITT

Feminist leader
Germany; 1855–1928

After a brief career as an actress, Marie Stritt began to concentrate on the women's question, no doubt inspired by her mother, who had been engaged in the Dresden's women's movement in the early 1890s, and eventually became a feminist leader in Germany.

Stritt was pioneering in her beliefs. She campaigned for birth control and abortion—an imprisonable offense of up to five years. Despite her efforts, however, more religiously conservative factions of the women's movement in Germany prohibited any real attempt to change the law (and indeed reflected a wider exclusionary nature toward radical feminism within the German women's movement).

Stritt also campaigned against state-sanctioned prostitution, inspired by British campaigner Josephine Butler (page 36) and she was a leading member of the League for the Protection of Motherhood and Sexual Reform. In 1894, she founded the Women's Legal Aid Society, before joining forces with Anita Augspurg, and merged into the Federation of German Women Association, eventually becoming elected as president. She was also the president of the National Women's Council for Germany, appearing at conferences around the world, and she joined the board of the International Woman Suffrage Alliance. The war interrupted Stritt's efforts but suffrage was finally granted to women in Germany in 1919.

CLARA ZETKIN

Communist sister
Germany; 1857–1933

On March 8 people around the world celebrate International Women's Day and that is largely thanks to Clara Zetkin.

Zetkin, a German Marxist and active member of the Social Democratic Party, suggested the idea at the International Conference of Working Women, in Copenhagen in 1911, in order to draw attention to the demands of working-class women. After initially being celebrated by Austria, Denmark, Germany and Switzerland, it eventually spread round the world and is still observed today.

Zetkin was a communist, not a feminist. She rejected feminism on the basis that it was a middle- and upper-class "bourgeois" movement that ignored the plights of the masses. She was, however, supportive of women's suffrage and was instrumental in the women's movement within the SDP, editing the women's newspaper and heading up the first Women's Office. Some have cited Zetkin as being one of the first German socialists to link the call for women's emancipation with the socialist movement. In 1920 Zetkin even interviewed Lenin on the subject: "Comrade Lenin frequently spoke to me about the women's question. Social equality for women was, of course, a principle needing no discussion for communists."

ANITA AUGSPURG

Peacemaker
Germany; 1857–1943

Anita Augspurg was as radical as she looked, with her shortly cropped hair and unconventional clothes.

Germany's first female lawyer, she was involved with the women's rights movement, championing radical, free lifestyles for women and likening marriage to prostitution. She was also heavily involved in the pacifist movement, drawing a link between the violence of patriarchal structures and the oppression of women (it's recently come to light that she requested Hitler's expulsion as early as 1923).

In a culmination of her beliefs, in 1915 she co-organized the International Congress of Women celebrated in The Hague. From this the Women's International League for Peace and Freedom was born—an organization that is still active today, promoting peaceful methods to ensure justice for women. And the newly introduced Anita Augspurg Award recognizes exceptional women working for peace around the world.

22   1

Az

Anna Maria
Mozzoni

ANNA MARIA MOZZONI

Radical fighter for emancipation
Italy; 1837–1920

Anna Maria Mozzoni was a radical, and is widely regarded as the founder of modern Italian feminism.

She founded the Socialist League in Milan in 1881, and vehemently opposed the traditional roles imposed upon women by the Catholic Church—what they believed to be sacred, she believed to be oppressive. She argued for women's civic and political rights to be recognized in the light of the *risorgimento*—the Italian unification, a process Mozzoni believed wouldn't be truly realized until women could fully exercise their liberty. In 1877, she presented a petition to the Italian government calling for suffrage and led the fight for what became known as women's "emancipation"—a word that drew on connotations of slavery in the United States, demanding women's educational and civic equality.

Mozzoni was also a prominent voice in the explosion of journals published at this time, used as megaphones for the feminist cause in Italy. In 1864 she wrote *Woman and her social relationships on the occasion of the revision of the Italian Civil Code,* and in 1879, she translated John Stuart Mill's *The Subjection of Women.*

Mozzoni died in 1920, two years before Mussolini came to power. Once at the helm, Mussolini reversed many of the hard-fought battles won by Mozzoni and her allies. Women were forced back into traditional roles and didn't receive the vote until 1945.

MARIA DERAISMES

Feminist intellectual
France; 1828–1894

Toward the end of the Second Empire in France, feminism came to the surface and was led by Maria Deraismes.

Deraismes was born into an open-minded middle-class family, who gave their daughters the education normally only reserved for sons, and while Deraismes originally harbored dreams of becoming a painter, as a young woman she found her voice as both a gutsy writer and a brilliant orator.

Her Paris salon became a haven of feminist thought and center of liberal opposition to Napoleon III. She gave lectures that drew big crowds, calling for the emancipation of women, and was also the first female freemason, a relationship she forged due to shared anti-clerical beliefs. With the help of Léon Richer, a key ally of the feminist movement, in 1866, the feminist group Société pour la *Revendication du Droit des Femmes* was founded, along with its own newspaper. In 1870, Deraismes founded *L'Association pour le droit des femmes*. While her work was interrupted by both the Franco-Prussian War and the Paris Commune uprising, when able to, she would tirelessly continue with her lectures, her writings and spreading her message of rights for women.

CLARA CAMPOAMOR

influential political voice
Spain; 1888–1972

Clara Campoamor was one of the most influential feminist voices in Spanish politics.

Born into a working-class family in Madrid, Campoamor's father died when she was just a child. After his death, she worked as a seamstress from the age of 13. She still, however, managed to pursue her education, first working as a teacher, as well as writing for liberal journal *La Tribuna,* where she began to develop her political ideas. She eventually became a lawyer, qualifying at the age of 36.

Campoamor dedicated her life to advocating women's rights. She worked on cases concerning marriage, paternity and child labor rights and became increasingly involved with feminist groups. When it became legal for women to run for the Constituent Assembly in 1931, which would draw up the new constitution for Spain's Second Republic, Campoamor was elected to the commission.

In her new role, she pushed for women to have the same rights as men and made some of the most progressive legislation in the world at the time. She was also the first woman to give a speech in front of the Constituent Assembly, and successfully fought for women's suffrage, which was passed under the new constitution in 1931.

Campoamor fled Spain on the outbreak of the civil war (1936–1939). Under General Franco's autocratic rule of Spain, which lasted until his death in 1975, women's rights were severely impeded.

See also: Victoria Kent

A name often associated with Clara Campoamor is Victoria Kent, another member of the Socialist Radical Party, and also a lawyer, elected to the assembly at the same time. Kent did not believe women were ready to be given the vote because she thought they would push for more conservative politics, governed by the power and sway of the Church. Campoamor disagreed. After a heated debate on October 1, 1931, Campoamor was crowned victor and suffrage was granted in the form of Article 36. On the outbreak of war, Kent worked in Paris aiding refugees from Spain. In 1950 she moved to New York where she worked for the UN and launched *Iberica,* a magazine opposed to Franco and communism in Spain.

LUCÍA SÁNCHEZ SAORNIL

Radical anarchist
Spain; 1895–1970

Lucía Sánchez Saornil held radical, anarchist views and dedicated her life to social revolution.

Her views sprang from when she was working as a telephonist. Her union organized a strike and Sánchez Saornil was deeply affected. By 1933, she was appointed the general secretary of the Solidaridad Internacional Antifascista (SIA)—an antifascist group.

Soon, however, she felt that the male anarchist movement did not embrace the female cause strongly enough, often ignoring the oppression of domesticity and Catholic ideals imposed upon women. Sánchez Saornil strove to fight the "double struggle" of women's liberation and social revolution. And so, along with two other women's groups, Sánchez Saornil formed the Mujeres Libres in 1936. The group ran lessons for working-class women who couldn't read or write, they published a newspaper, offered daycare programs and provided women-only spaces to discuss political ideas.

With the collapse of the Second Republic, the Civil War and the eventual return of the power of the Church and conservatism, the radical ideas of anarchy, and especially feminist-anarchists like Sánchez Saornil, were heavily clamped down on. Sánchez Saornil and her partner fled Spain, eventually settling in Argentina.

Although Sánchez Saornil may have felt her cause had failed, the Mujeres Libres are remembered for offering a radical alternative for the lives of working-class women.

"We want to write anew the word woman/ Fists upraised/ Women of the world toward horizons pregnant with light/ On paths afire onward, onward toward the light."

(from the lyrics of the Mujeres Libres anthem)

Lucía Sánchez Saornil

HE XIANGNING

Crusading nationalist
China; 1878–1972

First and foremost, Xiangning was a revolutionary.

She was one of the earliest members of Sun Yat-sen's revolutionary movement Tongmenghui (her husband was Sun Yat-sen's closest friend), also known as the Chinese Revolutionary Alliance, a secret resistance network. Later on in her life she worked to organize resistance against the Japanese invasion of China, and in 1928, she co-founded the Revolutionary Committee of the Chinese Kuomintang.

He Xiangning was also as strident in her feminism—even from an early age. Unlike most girls, Xiangning refused to have her feet bound. Her father eventually relented and married her to a Chinese-American who preferred her unbound "big feet."

She was appointed Minister for Women's Affairs under Sun's nationalist government and she pushed for equal rights. Xiangning wanted to draw women into the Revolution and the department attempted to educate and prepare women to become leaders, offering three months' training and a degree, before being sent out to recruit more women. While she was at odds with other Chinese Nationalist feminists for wanting to engage with more traditional women, she led China's first rally for International Women's Day in 1924. Three years later, there were 25,000 marching women in Canton.

Xiangning remained active and committed to the People's Republic of China for her long life (she died aged 94), sitting as Vice Chairwoman of the National People's Congress and honorary chairwoman of the All-China Women's Federation.

All her life Xiangning placed the fight for women's rights firmly at the heart of her unwavering commitment to revolution and Chinese nationalism.

Epic Marches

1. **2017 Women's March**
   The day after Donald Trump was inaugurated as the President of the United States, 673 marches took place on all seven continents.

2. **International Women's Day March, Petrograd March 8, 1917**
   What started as an International Women's Day march in Petrograd on March 8, 1917 became the beginning of the Russian Revolution. As women filled the streets, men joined them. By the end of the afternoon, 100,000 workers had come out on strike.

3. **New York Shirtwaist Strike, November 24, 1909**
   Led by Clara Lemlich and the International Ladies' Garment Workers' Union, 20,000 mostly Jewish women walked out of the shirtwaist garment factories in New York in a strike that lasted for almost four months.

4. **Women's march on Pretoria, August 9, 1956**
   20,000 women marched on the union buildings to protest against pass laws that aimed to limit the movement of black people in South Africa. They sang "you strike a woman, you strike a rock."

5. **Icelandic women's strike, October 24, 1975**
   On this day, Iceland came to a standstill as 90 percent of the country's women went on strike—from both the office and the home—protesting against unfair wages and employment practices.

6. **March for the Equal Rights Amendment, Washington DC, 1978**

   Over 100,000 people marched for ratification of the Equal Rights Amendment in Washington DC, organized by the National Organization of Women.

7. **#NiUnaMenos—Argentina (and other parts of South America), October 20, 2016**

   "Not one less" is the translation of the South American hashtag that raises awareness around high femicide rates. In 2016, women took to the streets to make their voices heard.

8. **Poland anti-abortion strike, October 3**

   After 100,000 women, dressed in black, went on strike to protest against an abortion ban, the government rejected the bill.

9. **SlutWalk, April 2011, Toronto (First SlutWalk)**

   After a Canadian police officer suggested women stop dressing like sluts to avoid being victims, protests took place around the world against a culture of victim blaming.

10. **Anti-gang-rape march, India, January 2, 2013**

    After a student was gang-raped and murdered on a bus, women took to the streets to call for an end to sexual violence in India.

Epic Marches

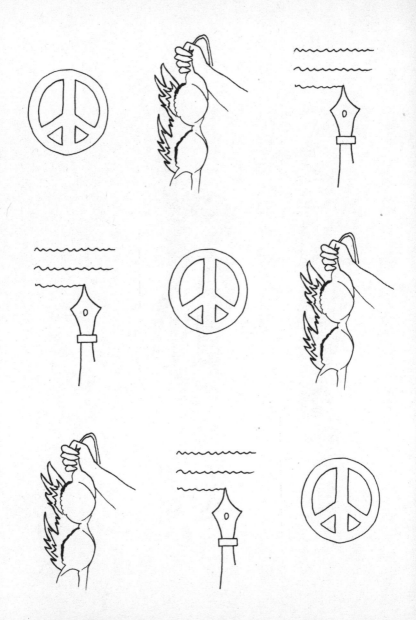

The
Second
Wave

Introducing:
The Second Wave

The 1960s and 1970s witnessed the transformation of a woman's place and purpose in the world. Her function, her worth, her self-determination, her right to choose, her economic and legal rights, her identity and her independence were revolutionized. It was a rebirth of what being a woman did and could mean. This was the Second Wave.

And it arrived after the 20th-century's greatest upheaval, two World Wars which left unspeakable devastation in their wake but also had provided women with an essential role in the war effort and in the workforce—many of whom had never worked before. Rosie the Riveter and her bicep became a symbol of women's economic power and their potential. In the windows between the wars, women were strong, capable and necessary. And as the world slowly got back up on its feet, it began to shift and change again. Revolutions in Russia and Argentina proved (at least to begin with) that the voice of the disenfranchised could be powerful and power could be shared. Women had entered the workforce en masse and weren't ready to down tools and disappear into domesticity again. The protests against the Vietnam War and the rise of the American Civil Rights Movement were transmitted on televisions for the world to see, infecting millions with the itch of resistance. The contraceptive pill and rock and roll created teenagers. Women and teenage girls could use their bodies to love freely and without responsibility. "The times they are a-changin'" sang Bob Dylan in 1964.

And so the drip, drip, dripping of change eventually caused the avalanche which was known as the women's liberation movement, and their demands were multiple. No more to the mindless existence of "the Angel of the House"; no more to back-street abortions in motel rooms on newspaper-covered floors; no more to the accepted violence of husbands who were to be obeyed; no more to the idea that women shouldn't or couldn't be lawyers or great philosophers or scientists or anything other than wives. Instead, women came together and they mobilized. They formed and reformed feminist organizations and caucuses and groups and collectives. From the radical to the religious and the creative, they raised their consciousness together, they shared their personal plight and turned it into political fuel together, they marched together, they protested together, they found their voices together.

In the 1960s, 70s and early 80s, women sought to reset the narrative: women aren't docile, they are dangerous. The Boston Women's Health Book Collective reeducated themselves on their own bodies, an area of expertise previously the preserve of men. Hélène Cixous, Luce Irigaray and Kate Millett reinterpreted the previously untouchable western canons of philosophy and culture and language and asked, "But where are the women, the real, actual, women?" Audre Lorde reaffirmed her identity, otherwise the patriarchy would do it for her—again. They revisited assumptions and revealed them as not natural truths but politics of oppression. And for many, their message was written down in pamphlets and books, in theories and manifestos, in essays and poetry and non-fiction. These women were writers. The revolution was written.

And like all revolutionaries, they fought with each other. They disagreed, disbanded and departed. The Second Wave, for many women of color, black women, lesbian women, disabled women, was a movement for a white, straight, middle-class women, not for them. Black women devised womanism as a way to speak to their own experiences; those who felt marginalized by the movement spoke in terms of intersectionality to show their oppression was not only on account of their gender. They saw how the politics of class, of sexuality and of race interconnected with gender and therefore they saw that feminism wasn't for them.

The women in this chapter questioned everything and they spoke truth to power. They were pioneers in the face of a tower of patriarchal status quo that kept women as Other, as sexualized objects, as obedient, as silent. They dismantled the myth of how the story of a woman's life should play out, and rewrote a reality that gave women freedom and made them the protagonists of their own lives. Yes, their revolution didn't reach all women— not by a long shot. Women and girls in the developing world, in oppressive regimes, in native and aboriginal communities, women of color, and working-class women didn't reap the rewards. It was, as many of the Third Wavers said, an incomplete mission. But they sure as hell created waves.

Once again, the nature of this book means that not all of the women who created the energy and power behind the revolution can be listed here. I sincerely hope that the women who are featured lead you to the women whose legacies live on in a world far bigger than our table.

All these women are our heroes—we owe them what rights we have today and we owe it to them to keep fighting. To the women of the Second Wave, we thank you.

SIMONE DE BEAUVOIR

Pioneering gender dismantler
France; 1908–1986

For many, there was one world before 38-year-old Simone de Beauvoir wrote *The Second Sex* in 1949 and an entirely different one after. As the *New York Times* wrote in 2010: "The Second Sex was an act of Promethean audacity—a theft of Olympic fire—from which there is no turning back."

De Beauvoir had set out to write a confessional essay as she'd become a newly established public writer. As she began to consider herself, she began to consider what it was to be a woman. After hours of reading "feminine mythology" she wrote, "It was a revelation. This world was a masculine world, my childhood was nourished by myths concocted by men."

The result was *The Second Sex*. The book has three main ideas: that men are everything, as she writes, "He is the Subject, he is Absolute, she is the Other"; that women's ultimate quest is not happiness but freedom; and, most famously, that "women are not born but made." De Beauvoir is considered a pioneer in making a distinction between sex and gender, whereby sex is rooted in biology and gender is a historical, social and political construct.

For many in the 1940s, de Beauvoir's feminism, in part inspired by the existentialism of her life-long partner Jean-Paul Sartre, was deeply shocking. The Vatican had the book put on the Index of Prohibited Books and she was accused of ridiculing France.

In the 1970s, de Beauvoir became involved with the women's lib movement. She spent time with the likes of Betty Friedan and Kate Millett and in 1971 she wrote and signed "The Manifesto of 343," in which women confessed to having illegal abortions.

Unfortunately, *The Second Sex* was originally translated into English by an American zoologist who accused de Beauvoir of "having verbal diarrhoea." The translation was grossly inaccurate and savagely cut. It wasn't until 2009 that an accurately translated edition was published. This itself proved de Beauvoir's theory—that the "Other" woman was voiceless in a man's world.

The Second Sex completely questioned the structural nature of power and in turn a woman's role in the world, and her

on ne naît
pas femme:
on le devient

Simone de Beauvoir
Quotation from Le deuxième sexe

capabilities. And not only did de Beauvoir articulate an inherent oppression, she recognized how this causes an identity crisis for women in a man's world. It was truly radical.

LUCE IRIGARAY

Ardent philosopher
Belgium; 1930–

A multi-disciplined intellectual, Luce Irigaray challenged the male perspective and dominance in the Western canon of philosophy and psychoanalytic thinking.

It's not easy or perhaps particularly appropriate to relay Irigaray's biography, as she believed the male-dominated academic establishment used personal information to undermine the work of challenging women, but it is important to note that she moved to Paris to study psychology in the 1960s and started attending lectures of Jacques Lacan.

In 1974, she published *Speculum of the Other Woman*. The book had an explosive reaction that saw Irigaray lose her university teaching position at the request of Lacan himself.

Irigaray had criticized not only Lacan, but Freud, Plato, Descartes and Hegel—no shy undertaking. She claimed that in all their philosophy and theory, what constitutes the ego, the experience of being, is always seen through a male perspective. She also, crucially, criticized the fact that their ideas of self-made male identity ignored the fact that the male self had a nurturing, influential, essential mother. Irigaray called this "cultural matricide" and in 1981 she wrote, "All western culture rests on the murder of the mother." Feminist Jane Clare Jones wrote in the *New Statesman*, "Her writing made me aware of the gaping absence in our culture of representations of female sexuality not shaped by the needs, desires and gaze of men."

In 1977, Irigaray published *This Sex Which Is Not One*, which expanded on these themes, as well as applying Marxist ideas of capital, commodity and transaction to a woman's place in society.

Irigaray was also known for her theory of "sexual difference," which has been criticized for essentialist notions of gender. She has been ridiculed by male thinkers such as Richard Dawkins for her gendering of philosophy, science and law. Yet Irigaray's contribution to feminist theory is important: she shook the very foundations of philosophical thinking. And even in today's light, her work forces us to continue to reconsider how we see ourselves in the world—through our own filters and those of others.

26   2
Hex
Hélène
Cixous

HÉLÈNE CIXOUS

Creator of a feminist language
France; 1937–

Hélène Cixous is known as the mother of post-structuralist feminist theory. A fierce intellectual and prolific writer, including poetry, plays, literary criticism and philosophy, she is deemed one of the heavyweights of both French intellectualism and feminism. In 1974, she founded the first center of feminist studies in Europe at the University of Paris VIII, and in 1975 she published *The Laugh of the Medusa*, which became a key text in feminist scholarship and introduced a radical new understanding of the relationship between language and sexuality.

It was here that Cixous created "*écriture féminine*"—a writing style that infused and inscribed the experience of the feminine body into language. It was, for Cixous, a rejection of the binary domination of patriarchy (man vs woman) which left woman as the Other. Instead, Cixous argued for a new language for women to express themselves in, free from the oppressive restraints of patriarchal dominance echoed in the structure of existing language. Cixous' écriture féminine was a mixture of the creative with the academic, including both dense theory and colloquialisms. It was made up of fragmented syntax and flowing, open, endless verse. It resisted the order, linear form and authority of the male-created language, which, she believes, does not allow women to truly write and speak their experience.

Cixous wrote:

> Woman must write herself; must write about women and bring women to writing from which they have been driven away as from their bodies—for the same reason, by the same laws, with the same fatal goal.

> (from "The Laugh of the Medusa")

"Woman must put herself into the text—as into the world and into history—by her own movement"

Hélène Cixous

MONIQUE WITTIG

Avant-garde novelist
France; 1935–2003

Monique Wittig was a pioneering radical lesbian feminist who expressed her feminism through experimental, often utopian novels, often devoid of men and made up of a completely avant-garde style of language.

Her first novel, *L'Opoponax*, published in 1964, told the story of a rebellious young girl in a convent and won the Prix Médicis literary award. The novel, in which the schoolgirls refer to themselves in the third person, was received by critics as a radical take on child consciousness. Her next novel, *Les Guérillères*, was described by Sally Beaman in the *Times Book Review* as "perhaps the first epic celebration of women ever written." Here, too, the language was, at times, completely deconstructed, with a giant "O" appearing on pages.

Margaret Reynolds of the *Guardian* wrote that every page is "a call to arms: the women affirming triumph that all action is overthrow." This was followed by *Le Corps Lesbien* in 1973 and *Virgile, Non* in 1983—both similarly experimental and promoting a radical notion of womanhood.

Wittig rejected the larger structures, too; she had a distaste for identity politics—something very much at odds with her contemporaries. She even famously said "Lesbians aren't women," because they do not exist under the patriarchal rule of a sexist society. She rejected the notion of women's literature, too—even though she helped to create a women's studies department at the University of Arizona where she taught in later life.

Wittig was praised by the elder French feminist community, including de Beauvoir and Marguerite Duras, and was recognized by many as one of the leading lights of the Second Wave movement. She became a founding member of the Mouvement de Libération des Femmes, and helped organize a separatist group called the Féministes Révolutionnaires.

Her writing was unapologetically daring, women-focused and original. She imagined a lesbian paradise for women that helped shape a new narrative and mythology. She was pioneering, visionary and totally unique.

5   2

Bf

Betty
Friedan

BETTY FRIEDAN

Housewife liberator
USA; 1921–2006

"The problem with no name" is how Betty Friedan, the journalist-turned-housewife, described the ailment that was bringing misery and despair to millions of women like her. In 1963, Friedman wrote *The Feminine Mystique*, and for many this marked the beginning of the women's liberation movement.

Friedan diagnosed the discontent of women whose opportunities had been subsumed by the expectation of domestic lives, women whose intellect and creativity lost out to society's demand that their chief purpose was as wife, mother and homemaker. A woman's worth was locked in the four walls of the home, which became a prison, or as Friedan controversially suggested, a concentration camp.

Friedan's book caused a huge stir at the time of publication. It released a genie that could never be put back in the bottle and was giving women the permission to ask for more than what society had previously allowed them. On the momentum of her book, Friedan went on to become a face of the Second Wave. She was one of the founders of the National Organization for Women and served as their first president from 1966 to 1970. She established the National Association for the Repeal of Abortion Laws and helped create the National Women's Political Caucus in 1971 along with Gloria Steinem (page 86), a country-wise, bipartisan, grassroots membership organization, in response to the fact that less than 1 percent of elected officials at the time were female. By the time of her death, *The Feminine Mystique* had sold three million copies.

In time, however, revisionist theories began to grow around Friedan's writing. In 1984, bell hooks (page 90) criticized Friedan, writing that she "did not discuss who would be called in to take care of the children and maintain the home if more women like herself were freed from their house labor and given equal access with white men to the professions ... she ignored the existence of all non-white women and poor white women."

While hooks' criticism is legitimate and became a crucial refrain in the failings of the women's movement, it is unquestionable that Friedan articulated a feeling that unlocked an era-defining movement. The floodgates opened after Friedan committed women's "problem with no name" to paper—and named it.

ADRIENNE RICH

Poet of the desperate housewives
USA; 1929–2012

Adrienne Rich put the struggles of the Second Wave into verse.

Rich articulated the misery of being a woman in a world dominated by men, stripped of ambition and trapped in domesticity. Her poetry reflected the situations of millions of American women who wanted more from life. In the title poem from *Snapshots of a Daughter-in-Law*, a collection of poetry published in 1963, she plunged deeply into the souls and psyches of many an American housewife.

On her death, the *New York Times* wrote: "She accomplished in verse what Betty Friedan did in prose. In describing the stifling minutiae that had defined women's lives for generations, both argued persuasively that women's disenfranchisement at the hands of men must end." In 1976, she published the non-fiction book *Of Woman Born*, a brutally honest examination of what it meant to be a mother, which British feminist Julie Bindel has called "a classic feminist text."

After a brief marriage, resulting in three sons, Rich came out as a lesbian in 1977 with the poetry collection *Twenty-One Love Poems*. In 1980, she published the essay "Compulsory Heterosexuality and Lesbian Existence"—an exploration of both lesbians in society, as well as lesbianism in relation to literary criticism.

Rich explored other elements of marginalized society, alongside gender and sexuality, such as her own Jewishness and the struggles of black women. When her poetry collection *Diving into the Wreck* won the National Book Award in

Your mind now,
moldering like
wedding cake,
heavy with useless
experience, rich
With suspicion,
rumor, fantasy,
crumbling to
pieces under the
knife edge of
mere fact."
(from the poem
"Snapshots of a
Daugher-in-Law")

Adrienne Rich

1974 (jointly with Allen Ginsberg), all the women nominated had made a pact that they would claim the prize together in a show of solidarity. Rich took to the stage alongside Audre Lorde (page 92) and Alice Walker (page 98) and read out a statement they had prepared together:

> We dedicate this occasion to the struggle for self-determination of all women, of every color, identification, or derived class: the poet, the housewife, the lesbian, the mathematician, the mother, the dishwasher, the pregnant teenager, the teacher, the grandmother, the prostitute, the philosopher, the waitress, the women who will understand what we are doing here and those who will not understand yet; the silent women whose voices have been denied us, the articulate women who have given us strength to do our work.

Rich's poetry is dazzling and innovative in its own right—but she made her poetry political and personal and the stories she told were the stories of a changing generation on the cusp of freedom. Gifted and brave, Rich wrote poetry that went beyond the arts; it helped change the world for the better.

MARIAROSA DALLA COSTA

Italian Marxist
Italy; 1943–

One of the key issues that came to shape the Second Wave was the debate around housework. Should women be paid for their labor in their own household? Many feminists thought they should, suggesting that their unpaid labor was yet another form of oppression under the patriarchy.

One of those feminists was the Italian-born Dalla Costa. Dalla Costa had experience in the Italian workers' Marxist movement, known as *operaismo*, which came out of factory strikes in the north of the country. She was also a member of the Lotta Femminista, a small faction of the Italian feminist movement, also inspired by those same "workerist" communist ideas.

After developing a political friendship with feminist Selma James, she organized a meeting in Padua in 1971 with James and others to share her ideas of a manifesto she'd drafted: women should be paid for their labor in the home. A year later, she co-founded the International Feminist Collective, which became the International Wages for Housework Campaign. The group was a feminist expression of anti-capitalist aims—to see women fairly remunerated and their labor no longer exploited. Together with James, she published *The Power of Women and the Subversion of the Community* in 1972.

By 1973, a chapter had launched in Brooklyn, New York, by Silvia Federici before spreading right across the States. Two years later, Federici published *Wages Against Housework*—the book that came to symbolize the movement. Other faces of the movement erupted, too—Black Women for Wages for Housework, Wages Due Lesbians, and WinVisible (women with visible and invisible disabilities).

While Mariarosa Dalla Costa's name might not be one of the most well-known of the Second Wave, she recognized a huge global inequality and began a very important conversation that was based on ideas of power, oppression and women's roles in society. She took the ideas of Marx and applied them specifically to the lives of women, recasting what had been perceived as an inherently feminine responsibility as a political form of oppression and exploitation, and boldly demanded compensation. In doing so, she challenged the status quo and elevated the lives of women to a political endeavor worth fighting for.

JAYABEN DESAI

Brave voice for immigrant women
UK; 1933–2010

On a hot August day in 1976, Indian-born Jayaben Desai walked out of the Grunwick film-processing plant in Willesden, north-west London, and went on strike. What followed was two years of strikes, with support from over 150 unions across the country. Cabinet ministers lent their support, the post office temporarily cut off the factory's mail and one picket during 1977 drew a crowd of 20,000 people.

Desai was a recent immigrant to London, having originally left India for Tanganyika with her husband, who was from the East African colony (now Tanzania and Zanzibar). She had always been politically engaged and outspoken, protesting for Indian independence as a schoolgirl. When she arrived in Britain and found herself underpaid and discriminated against, she was ready to speak out again.

The conditions in Grunwick were oppressive and the factory employed Asian immigrant women, assuming they could pay them less and work them harder. The women were forced to do over-time, had to ask permission to use the toilet, were paid 70p per hour (below the average wage) and were routinely humiliated by the factory manager. When one of her colleagues was fired for working too slowly, and Desai was issued a formal warning for refusing to do overtime, she had had enough. She reportedly told her manager, "What you are running is not a factory, it is a zoo. In a zoo, there are many types of animal. Some are monkeys who dance on your fingertips. Others are lions who can bite your head off. We are the lions, Mr. Manager."

After 23 months, the unions caved, the factory refused to rein-state sacked workers and the strike, to some, had failed. But all was not lost. In a story that feels prescient to our time, an immigrant had challenged a discriminatory authority and, through her brave actions, for a moment had led a movement with the support of tens of thousands of people. Challenging the stereotype of submissive Asian women and challenging the idea that immigrant women could be treated as second-class citizens, Desai's bravery was an important moment in the working rights of immigrant women.

90   **2**

Gg

Germaine
Greer

GERMAINE GREER

Feminist stimulant
Australia; 1939–

Germaine Greer is the outrageous, controversial, provocative and angry mother of women's liberation. On her 75th birthday, Helen Lewis of the *New Statesman* called her "feminism's arsonist" and Zohra Moosa described her like "lightning"—"though brilliant, she has also been painful and damaging to feminist movements." In 1970, Greer published *The Female Eunuch*, the bestselling polemic that turned Greer into a household name (on the cover of *Life* magazine in 1971, she was labelled the "saucy feminist that even men like"). The book calls for women to reject the oppression of nuclear family life and the submissive role that women play, to embrace their sexuality and to empower themselves with careers that men enjoy.

It was also full of radical ideas, directives and awakenings that Rosie Boycott, editor of the British feminist magazine *Spare Rib*, said "pushed back boundaries of being female, making our claustrophobic female world suddenly much, much bigger." These included encouraging women to taste their own menstrual blood and Greer's conviction that "women have very little idea of how much men hate them." *The Female Eunuch* shocked a generation of women into the awareness of their own oppression, calling for them to fight back. And Greer didn't want equality; she wanted liberation. As she wrote in *The Whole Woman*, the 1999 follow-up to *The Female Eunuch*: "Women's liberation did not see the female's potential in terms of the male's actual."

While she whipped women into a tornado of feminist anger, she has often come in for criticism from the feminist community, such as for her culturally relativist approach to FGM and transphobia, often stating her belief that transwomen are not women. She resigned from her position at Cambridge University after a trans woman professor joined her all-women college. This view has led her to be no-platformed by university students, accused of hate speech.

Greer's outspokenness, her incredible intellect and her confidence were a crucial power behind the women's movement

human beings
have an inalienable
right to invent
themselves

Germaine Greer
Quotation from an article in The Times, published in 1986

of the Second Wave. And while today the Fourth Wave often rejects her, she is an essential character in the story of feminism. Her refusal to kowtow to the views of anyone has surely not made for an easy ride, but Greer's fight paved a road that many could subsequently travel much more peacefully. As Helen Lewis continued, "The point of Greer is not to be constantly correct or make you feel better … she is a stimulant not a painkiller."

KATE MILLETT

Visionary feminist cultural critic
USA; 1934–2017

You've probably heard of Germaine Greer's *The Female Eunuch* and Betty Friedan's *The Feminine Mystique*, but have you heard of Kate Millet's *Sexual Politics*?

Why Millett isn't such a familiar name is perplexing, considering she wrote *Sexual Politics*, her dissertation at Columbia turned bestseller, published in 1970 and described by the *New York Times* that year as the "bible of women's liberation." On her death, Judith Shulevitz, of the *New York Review of Books,* wrote that despite being "half forgotten … you can't deny that Millett made reading a life-changing, even world-changing, act." So explosive was the book that Millett found herself on the cover of *Time*, with a banner reading, "The Politics of Sex."

In the book, Millett focuses on male thinkers and writers including Freud, D H Lawrence, Henry Miller and Norman Mailer, radically criticizing the literary canon for its depiction of women. She claimed the use of sex in their work was degrading to women and supported a patriarchal system that infects culture, literature and philosophy.

Millett became a committee member of the National Organization for Women in 1966, before joining more radical groups such as New York Radical Women. Millett continued to publish books on feminism throughout her life, covering issues of submission, torture, prostitution and of her time spent in Tehran. She also wrote a book about her own bisexuality and her experiences suffering from mental health problems. She became involved in radical feminist art groups, exhibiting her own works across the United States. In 2013 she was inducted into the Women's Hall of Fame.

In just one book, Millett shook the foundations of the literary canon and was instrumental in the creation of a new wave of feminism. She saw how the portrayal of women played into a politics of power and she called it out, awakening other women to what she had seen.

SHULAMITH FIRESTONE

Radical organizer
Canada; 1945–2012

Shulamith Firestone is the feminist's feminist. Kate Millett said of her, "I was taking on the obvious male chauvinists. Shulie was taking on the whole ball of wax. What she was doing was much more dangerous." Collette Price, an important part of the 1970s feminist New York scene, remarked "to us, she was the American Simone de Beauvoir." Even Simone de Beauvoir was impressed, telling *Ms.* magazine that Firestone had "started something new."

Shulamith Bath Shmuel Ben Ari Feuerstein (the family Americanized their name to Firestone when Shulamith was a child) was an art school student in Chicago when she started her first feminist group, but it was in 1967, when she moved to New York, that Firestone began to mold radical feminism and push the women's movement in a daring, challenging direction. In *The Dialectic of Sex: The Case for Feminist Revolution*, her hugely influential book written in 1970, aged just 25, she said, "Feminists have to question not just all of western culture but the organization of culture itself and further, even the organization of nature."

Firestone, or the aptly named "firebrand" or "fireball," adopted the theories of Marx, Engels, Freud and de Beauvoir into her own brand of radical feminist politics. She attacked the nuclear family for exploiting women's biological function as a means of oppression and envisioned a future where babies could be made in artificial wombs outside of the body, preventing women from having to be pregnant at all. "Pregnancy is barbaric," she wrote. "Childbirth is like shitting a pumpkin." She called for wider access to contraception and abortion, as well as "the elimination of not just male privilege but of the sex distinction itself."

In 1967, she co-founded New York Radical Women, the city's first women's liberation group. Famously, the group protested at the 1968 Miss America where they threw fake eyelashes and pots and pans into a "trash can of freedom" and unfurled a large banner emblazoned with "Women's Liberation."

Firestone started the Redstockings in 1969, and organized the nation's first abortion "speak out," for which she persuaded 12 women to talk publicly about their experience of abortion. One of those women was Gloria Steinem (below).

Feminist activist and academic Ann Snitow said that Firestone was "aflame, incandescent," but her radical spark disappeared as quickly as it arrived. Firestone became less active but continued to publish writings in the early 1970s before withdrawing from politics completely.

Firestone's story has a tragic ending: she was diagnosed with schizophrenia, and disassociated herself from her parents. Her body was found in her flat a week after she had died. This isolation in her later life was believed to be a by-product of her commitment to the women's movement, which itself had become internally fractured and externally ridiculed. Yet Firestone herself knew the fight for equality wouldn't be an easy path: "Many women give up in despair," she wrote in *The Dialectic of Sex*. "If that's how deep it goes, they don't want to know. Others continue strengthening and enlarging the movement. Their painful sensitivity to the female oppression existing for a purpose eventually to eliminate it." That was Shulamith Firestone.

GLORIA STEINEM

Writer, organizer, protester
USA; 1934–

With her signature big glasses and a steely determination, Steinem helped lead the women's rights "revolution" (as she called it). Inspired by attending civil rights movement rallies; time spent in India as a young woman; her own abortion and her mother's

a woman without a
man is like a fish
without a bicycle

Gloria Steinem
(quotation originally by Irina Dunn)

sacrifice of her career as a reporter to bring up Steinem and her sister, Steinem became a key organizer and voice of the Second Wave's fight for equality.

Steinem was a journalist by trade and wrote many articles that helped cement her status as a feminist voice, including her investigation into the exploitation of Playboy Bunnies and the 1969 "After Black Power, Women's Liberation." In 1972, along with Dorothy Pitman Hughes, Steinem founded Ms. magazine (which was originally going to be called Sojourner after Sojourner Truth, page 39). Steinem and Hughes were determined to create a publication for women, made by women, voicing taboo issues including abortion, domestic violence and FGM. The magazine advocated economic independence and interviewed pioneering women of the day—giving a voice, platform and engine to the movement.

Steinem was also one of the founders of the National Women's Political Caucus and gave a speech called "Address to the Women of America." Throughout her life she has supported the advancement of women, from helping female Democrats to run for office to addressing the first National Conference of Stewardesses for Women's Rights in New York City in 1973.

Since the 1960s, Steinem has been asked by the media to comment on issues of sexism. Even now—or perhaps especially now she's a woman in her 80s who has seen first-hand women's rights grow, flourish, and at times retract—Steinem's voice is an absolute authority.

The Second Wave is often (fairly) criticized for being a movement of the white middle classes. Indeed, Steinem has even had her appearance labelled a privilege. But Steinem's commitment to the movement is indisputable. At the coal face during one of the most transformative times for women's rights, Steinem pushed fearlessly for change. All women today who have access to abortion, the right to refuse to be battered by their partner, and the right to demand equal pay for equal work owe Gloria Steinem a huge debt of gratitude.

28 2

ANDREA DWORKIN

Sexual violence warrior
USA; 1946–2005

In the year the radical American feminist Andrea Dworkin died, filmmaker Havana Marking stingingly wrote that Dworkin's true legacy has been that "far too many young women today would rather be bitten by a rabid dog than be considered a feminist."

Marking's words might not be true, but they paint a picture of the stereotype Dworkin and feminism would start to take on in the 1980s and 1990s: hairy, make-upless, overweight, dungarees and DMs. Compounded by this, Dworkin was labelled a man hater; people accused her of suggesting all sex was rape.

Her views were radical and she was pushing feminist dialogue to its very limits. Her books, particularly *Woman Hating* (1974), *Pornography: Men Possessing Women* (1981) and *Intercourse* (1987), focused on issues of violence and sexual violence against women and girls. She denied suggesting all sex was rape, saying she meant the act had to be reciprocal and "not an act of aggression from a man looking only to satisfy himself." But her views weren't always easily digestible. She wrote, "Pornography is a celebration of rape and injury to women" and "I really believe a woman has the right to execute a man who has raped her."

Dworkin's extreme position may well have been born of her own experience. She was raped when she was nine, she was sexually assaulted by an internal inspection at Women's House of Detention in Greenwich, New York, where she was being held aged 18, leaving her bleeding for days and badly bruised. Her first husband was violent. And in 1999, she was drugged and raped.

Yet there are many who recognize Dworkin's contribution to feminism as essential. One of the most controversial feminists of the Fourth Wave, Jessa Crispin, has called for younger feminists to embrace Dworkin's militant approach. On her death, the now editor of the *Guardian*, Kath Viner, wrote, "She was a bedrock, the place to start from: even when you disagreed with her, her arguments were infuriating, fascinating, hard to forget. Feminism needs those who won't compromise, even in their appearance."

BELL HOOKS

Voice of a generation
USA; 1952–

bell hooks is one the most important voices to emerge from the women's liberation movement. Critiquing the intersection of gender, race, class and culture (or what she famously called the "imperialist white supremacist capitalist patriarchy"), hooks has published over 30 books that have made her a defining voice on the politics of black womanhood in America.

hooks, born Gloria Jean Watkins, was raised in Kentucky at the height of racial segregation. As she began her writing career, she renamed herself bell hooks after her outspoken great-grandmother. She used the decapitalization of her name to make the point that her writing was about her ideas and not her.

In 1981, hooks published what would become one of her— and the Second Wave's—most important texts, *Ain't I a Woman?: Black Women and Feminism*. The book examines the impact of slavery on black womanhood and takes an intersectional approach to black women's oppression. hooks considers sexism amongst black men, writing "Marcus Garvey, Elijah Muhammed, Malcolm X, Martin Luther King, Stokely Carmichael, Amiri Baraka and other black male leaders have righteously supported patriarchy." She also discusses racism from white women: "The process [of liberation] begins with the individual woman's acceptance that American women, without exception, are socialized to be racist, classist and sexist, in varying degrees."

In *Feminist Theory: From Margin to Center*, published in 1984, hooks defined feminism as "a movement to end sexism, sexist exploitation and oppression"—a definition she stood by again in *Feminism Is for Everybody*, published in 2000, saying she liked this definition because it did not imply men were the enemy, an argument that can be found throughout her writing.

Like many of her Second Wave sisters, today hooks' voice is seen as controversial yet important. In 2014, she called Beyoncé "a terrorist"—referring to the idea that "perfect"

bell hooks

images of the singer bombard young women and make them feel inadequate. Whether or not you agree with her is irrelevant. hooks is still challenging women—as she has always done—to understand the root of their oppression and their true value in the world.

AUDRE LORDE

Political black lesbian warrior wordsmith
USA; 1934–1992

Audre Lorde was a poet, a feminist, a lesbian, a "warrior," a black mother, a teacher and a librarian.

Her many identities—the existence, and the agonies and the ecstasy of them—were the subject of her poetry, essays and speeches. For Lorde, naming her multitudes was a form of political control, a rewriting of a narrative. As she once said, "If I didn't define myself, I would be crunched by other people's fantasies and eaten alive."

Born to immigrant Caribbean parents in New York City in 1934, Audre dropped the "y" from her first name as a child and began writing poetry. As an adult, she became a librarian while continuing to write. She published her first collection of poetry, *The First Cities*, in 1968 and became poet-in-residence at Tougaloo College, Mississippi.

Lorde took human experiences and turned them into political weaponry; poetry was the expression of black womanhood. As she wrote in her essay "Poetry Is Not a Luxury," "The white fathers told us: I think therefore I am. The Black mother within each of us—the poet—whispers: I feel therefore I can be free."

Silence was Lorde's greatest enemy. Silence allowed injustice, racism and sexism. We have to speak out, she urged:

What are the words you do yet have? What do you need to say? What are the tyrannies you swallow day by day in an attempt to make your own, until you will sicken and die of them, still in silence? Because I am here today, I am the face of one of your fears.

Because I am woman, because I am Black, because I am lesbian, because I am myself, a Black woman warrior poet doing my work—come to ask you, are you doing yours?

Lorde's writings for justice ring true today. She called for intersectionality, and championed self-care long before it became an Instagram affirmation: "Caring for myself is not self-indulgence, it is self-preservation, and that is an act of political warfare."

Her life was cut short. She died of cancer in 1992, but Lorde's body of work is both timeless and prescient, offering generations a language of resistance. As she wrote, "there are no new ideas; there are only new ways of making them felt." Reading Audre Lorde is like lightning in your veins, a new way of feeling.

"I am not free
while any woman
is unfree, even
when her shackles
are very different
from my own."

Audre Lorde
(from the speech "The Uses of Anger: Women Responding to
Racism" given in 1981)

FRIDA KAHLO

Selfie-queen and rediscovered icon
Mexico; 1907–1954

Before the 1970s, Frida Kahlo was primarily known as the wife of the world-famous muralist Diego Rivera. She had only two solo international exhibitions of her work, one in New York in 1938, one in Paris in 1939. She exhibited for the first time in Mexico, her home country, in 1953, just a year before her death. But thanks to the growing women's movement, which placed a renewed interest in women and women of color in the arts, she was revisited as an artist in her own right. Between 1978 and 1979, six U.S. museums featured retrospectives of her work. Today she is heralded as one of the most important female artists of the 20th century.

Kahlo's subject was herself—a radically feminist act in itself according to many critics, escaping the oppressive male gaze. And in her self-portraits she rejected convention, celebrating what she called her "beautiful ugly" and emphasizing her connected dark brows.

She told the story of pain in her work—a central theme of her life. She had polio as a child and at 18 she was involved in a traffic accident, leaving her unable to have children. Her pictures revealed the physical and psychological pain she experienced, depicting the taboo subjects of miscarriage, abortion and sexuality.

Both Kahlo and Rivera had many affairs throughout their marriage. But while some have questioned her feminism for staying with Rivera and seemingly spending her life in the shadow of his alleged genius, others celebrate her candid confrontation of physical and emotional pain as empowering. Madonna, who owns two of her paintings, has said she admires her "courage to reveal what a lot of people choose to hide in feelings of being unworthy." Feminist artist Miriam Schapiro has said,

pies para que
los quiero si
tengo alas
para volar

Frida Kahlo
Quotation from a diary illustration in 1954

Frida is a real feminist artist in the sense that during a period in history when the accepted modes of truth were truth seen through men's eyes, she gave us truth seen through the eyes of woman. She painted the kinds of agonies women in particular suffer, and she had the capacity both to be feminine and to function with an iron will that we associate with masculinity.

92 2

Jc

Judy Chicago

JUDY CHICAGO

Putting feminist art on the map
USA; 1939–

When the revered art critic Hilton Kramer saw Judy Chicago's 1979 mega-sculpture *The Dinner Party*, he was less than impressed: "Very bad art," he said. "Failed art ... art so mired in the pieties of a cause that it quite fails to capture any independent artistic life of its own."

This pious cause he so condescendingly mocked was feminism, and today *The Dinner Party* is perceived as one of the great feminist artworks of the century.

The Dinner Party consists of a large triangle, with 39 place settings arranged along the sides, each for a woman from history, from the goddesses of the classical world to Virginia Woolf and Susan B Anthony. The names of women are embroidered on the tablecloth and each place is laid with a plate displaying a painted vaginal form. Chicago wanted to tell the story of women in art and in history, a story she believed had been deliberately erased.

Feminism had always been core to Chicago. Born Judy Cohen, Chicago changed her name to her hometown as a feminist statement—a rejection of being identified by a relationship to a man. As a student at UCLA, she exhibited *Bigamy*, a series of male and female sex organs, and for her final piece she created *Car Hood*, a series of vaginal shapes spraypainted onto the—in her words—"masculine" hood of a 1960s car, a skill she'd learned from enrolling in an auto-body school, the only woman out of 250 men.

In 1971, she began teaching at Fresno State College. In the spring of the following year, she launched the Feminist Art Program, the first of its kind in the United States, in which Chicago would encourage women to talk about their lives and the experience of being a woman to help inform their art. A year later she moved to the California Institute of the Arts and co-founded Womanhouse with Miriam Schapiro, an exhibition space to display a female point of view.

Chicago continues to make art and today has been rightfully recognized as one of the most important feminist artists of her generation.

ALICE WALKER

Poet, author and creator of Womanism
USA; 1944–

Poet, author and feminist Alice Walker has been an activist since she turned down a scholarship to Paris to return to her place of birth, the American Deep South, to help aid the civil rights movement. (During this time she met and married a civil rights attorney who was white. Inter-racial marriage was illegal in Mississippi. She later said, "I proposed to him. I don't believe in marriage, I did it because it was illegal.")

Walker started publishing poetry while also working at *Ms.* magazine with Steinem, contributing from 1974 to 1986. In 1975 she published an article on the forgotten black writer Zora Neale Hurston, which recounts Walker's efforts to piece together details of her life and track down her unmarked grave. When she found it, she had a headstone placed there, reading "genius of the south." Walker's dedication to Hurston's legacy is part of a lifelong tribute to black women and their creativity.

In 1982, Walker wrote *The Color Purple*, which became a Pulitzer Prize–winning novel (making Walker the first woman of color to receive the award), a film directed by Steven Spielberg, and went on to appear on many school syllabi.

"Activism is the rent I pay for living on this planet"

Alice Walker

A year later she wrote *In Search of Our Mothers' Gardens*, a selection of essays in which she coins the term "womanism"—feminism that speaks directly to the experience of black women, once saying "womanism is to feminism what purple is to lavender." While Walker went on to contradict herself on the definition of the phrase and feminist scholars have since debated the exact meaning within feminist theory, womanism has become synonymous with finding a language for black feminists who often felt excluded from the white women's liberation movement.

52   2
Cl
Carla Lonzi

CARLA LONZI

Art critic–turned–feminist
Italy; 1931–1982

"Carla Lonzi is perhaps the most important feminist of her generation in Italy." This is what the organizers of an exhibition of Lonzi's work, Suite Rivolta—Carla Lonzi's feminism and the art of revolt—that opened in Lisbon in 2015, said of the art critic–turned–feminist.

Lonzi's career change happened when she realized she could no longer reconcile the patriarchal art world with her feminist principles. In 1970, she co-founded Rivolta Femminile, a feminist collective who wrote their manifesto on the walls of Rome in the summer of that year. Their group was based on the practice of *autocoscienza*—self-awareness or conscious raising. However, for Lonzi, autocoscienza was only fully achieved when recognized by another woman. It was a collective experience.

In the early 1970s, Lonzi published works that went on to become seminal Italian feminist texts. These include *Let's Spit on Hegel* in 1970, which attacked the patriarchal nature of his work. This was followed by *Clitoral Woman and Vaginal Woman* in 1971, whereby Lonzi examined the political nature of female sexuality via the writings of Freud and the Kama Sutra. Lonzi claimed that the myth of the vaginal orgasm was used to maintain male dominance, and the "clitoral woman" was a woman who had sexual pleasure on her own terms, outside of the demands of serving a male-dominated society. Her third book, *Diary of a Feminist*, included personal entries from 1972–1977, which Lonzi used as a consciousness raising act in itself.

Lonzi was radical both in terms of her politicisation of sexuality but also in the form it took—using diary entries and conversations to transmit her fight for equality.

ALICE SCHWARZER

Tireless editor
Germany; 1942–

"Had someone told me 40 years ago that I would still be doing *EMMA* in the year 2017, I would probably have just shaken my head in disbelief."

This is Alice Schwarzer, Germany's most prominent feminist on the pioneering feminist magazine she founded in January 1977, funded with the money she'd made as a bestselling author, and that she has edited ever since.

This was by no means Schwarzer's first foray into feminist activism. As a young woman she'd spent time in Paris, where she joined the Movement for the Liberation of Women in 1970, and began to meet with the stars of the city's intellectual set, including Jean-Paul Sartre and Simone de Beauvoir (page 70). A year later, she joined de Beauvoir, Catherine Deneuve and 340 other women in publicly admitting they'd had abortions. It was a tactic that was part of a successful campaign to have abortion legalized in France.

In 1971, Schwarzer returned to Germany and began to spread the feminism she had witnessed and been part of. She echoed the actions of de Beauvoir and launched Women Against Section 218, which saw women take to the streets and publicly declare that they had had an illegal abortion.

For four decades, *EMMA* has been Germany's feminist voice and Schwarzer has continued to campaign on issues such as pornography, what she believes is the oppression of the burqa and the revival of anti-abortion sentiment in Germany and other parts of Europe. "I have been speaking out now for almost 50 years," she told the *New York Times* in 2017.

Schwarzer continues as the foremost authoritative feminist voice in Germany and shows no signs of slowing down. Plus, there are still reasons to be hopeful. About the appointment of Angela Merkel as Chancellor she said, "I almost wept … Yes, now little girls in Germany know they can become a hairdresser, or chancellor."

BARBARA SMITH

Publishing pioneer
USA; 1946–

Barbara Smith was determined to give black women writers their seat at the table.

Although Smith was just nine when her mother died, her mother's education and love of books were fed passionately to her daughters. Smith became a ferocious reader and excellent student. Her passion for education continued and she went to postgrad school so she could eventually teach African-American literature. When she got there, she realized there were no African-American women on the syllabus. She said, "Black studies and black literature was about black male experience and women's studies was very much about white women's experience."

So in 1973, Smith taught the first class on black women's literature at Emerson College, Boston. She has said, "Every new day was a revelation. We were learning about ourselves." Smith's pursuit to celebrate black women's writing went further. In 1980, she co-founded the Kitchen Table: Women of Color Press—the first U.S. publisher dedicated to women of color. Smith was also keen to publish lesbian women. Smith has no doubt of the impact her publishing house had: "We really made an impact on mainstream publishing. You saw more and more women of color; Amy Tan, Toni Morrison and Alice Walker and that was because of us."

Smith and her twin sister Beverly were also committed activists in the civil rights movement, starting in high school, when they attended rallies and heard Martin Luther King speak. She was involved with Students for a Democratic Society activities before joining the National Black Feminist Organization in New York City in 1973, and eventually setting up the Boston chapter of the group. A few years later, Smith broke away and set up her own socialist black feminist group called Combahee River Collective.

Smith was a pioneering woman of color who was determined to give other women like her a voice—and to publish books in which readers could see a reflection of their own. Today, Smith works with the Florida mayor's office on violence prevention and social justice, and also lectures: "I meet young black women who think there's nothing wrong with the way they look, the way they sound ... because they do look out and see their faces reflected in places we did not."

PAULI MURRAY

Understated social justice pioneer
USA; 1910–1985

Fifteen years before Rosa Parks was arrested for refusing to give up her seat, Anna Pauline Murray (or Pauli, as she preferred to be called) was arrested in Virginia for refusing to move to the back of a bus. This was just one of the many remarkable things Murray did in her often-forgotten life.

The Baltimore-born orphan raised by her aunt went on to form the basis of some of the most progressive legislation in the two great social justice movements of the 20th century: civil rights and women's liberation. Her final-term law school paper was used by the legal team in the landmark *Brown v Board of Education* case (the Supreme Court ruling that segregated schools were unconstitutional). Later on in her legal career, she wrote a law review article used by the formidable Ruth Bader Ginsburg (page 106) in the high-profile *Reed* case, which would be the first time that the Equal Protection Clause of the Fourteenth

Amendment had been used to revoke a law that discriminated against women. As Kathryn Schulz wrote in the *New Yorker*, it was "Murray's lifelong fate to be both ahead of her time and behind the scenes."

As an adult, Murray rejected the segregation she had witnessed growing up—be it based on race or gender. When enrolled in Howard law school, she found herself the only female in a class with a mocking professor. She named this experience "Jane Crow"—a play on the heinous and racist Jim Crow laws and the intersectionality of her oppression. Brittney Cooper of *Slate* has written that Murray was a forerunner to Kimberlé Crenshaw: "Pauli Murray's initial invocation of the race-sex analogy for black women's positionality within the law that is the most direct precursor to Crenshaw's theory of intersectionality." In 1966, Murray co-founded the National Organization for Women with Betty Friedan.

The list of Murray's achievements is long. She became friends with Eleanor Roosevelt after writing to FDR about the injustice of a trial against a black sharecropper. She was appointed to President John F. Kennedy's Commission on the Status of Women, and at the end of her life she became the first African-American woman to be ordained a priest in the Protestant Episcopal Church in 1977.

Murray's incredible story is coming slowly back into the light after the publication of two new books about her life in 2017, and Yale has named a college after her. In *Jane Crow: The Life of Pauli Murray*, her biographer, Rosalind Rosenberg, explores Murray's often hidden lesbian relationships and private expression to change her gender, believing she was more aligned to being a man than a woman.

Now a shimmer of recognition is slowly starting to shine on Murray, we must make sure she is never forgotten again.

91   2
Fk
Florynce
Kennedy

FLORYNCE KENNEDY

Outrageous, outspoken lawyer
USA; 1916–2000

Florynce Kennedy is "the biggest, loudest and indisputably the rudest mouth on the battleground where feminists and radical politics join in mostly common cause." This is how *People* magazine described the lawyer, organizer, activist and feminist—"Flo," as she was known—in 1974.

By this time, Kansas City–born Kennedy had made waves within the feminist movement. When Columbia Law School refused her admission, she threatened to sue. When she was eventually admitted she was one of eight women and the only black person in her class.

In 1966, she was one of the founders of the National Organization for Women, and in the same year she represented civil rights leader H Rap Brown and started the Media Workshop to call out racism in advertising and the press. In 1968, she sued the Catholic Church for what she described as interference with abortion. A year later she organized a group of women lawyers to challenge New York abortion laws as well as helping to represent 21 members of the Black Panthers on trial. In 1971, she founded the Feminist Party and supported Shirley Chisholm as a 1972 presidential candidate. She also represented the radical feminist Valerie Solanas, who was charged with the attempted murder of Andy Warhol.

Her ferocious drive and determination were matched in scale by her larger-than-life personality, donning a pink cowboy hat, sunglasses and fake eyelashes. Gloria Steinem has said that Kennedy understood that "there has to be laughter and fun at the revolution, or it isn't a revolution."

But behind the noise and flamboyance, Flo Kennedy had an extremely important mission:

My main message is that we have a pathologically, institutionally racist, sexist, classist society. And that niggerizing techniques that are used don't only damage black people, but they also damage women, gay people, ex–prison inmates, prostitutes, children, old people, handicapped people, and native Americans.

RUTH BADER GINSBURG

Pioneering feminist lawyer
USA; 1933–

Octogenarian Associate Justice of the Supreme Court Ruth Bader Ginsburg is a pioneering legal powerhouse and, in her own words, a "flaming feminist litigator."

RBG's ascent to becoming Supreme Court Judge in 1993 reflects the women's rights story of the 20th century. When Ginsberg was a student at Harvard Law School, the dean asked her and the eight other female students, "How do you justify taking a spot from a qualified man?" Newly qualified, she was refused a clerical role because of her gender. She had to hide her second pregnancy for fear of losing her tenure, and after discovering she did not earn the same as her male counterparts at Rutgers School of Law, she led a successful campaign for equal pay.

But these hurdles did not deter RBG. In 1970, she co-launched the *Women's Rights Law Reporter*, the first law journal in the U.S. to focus exclusively on women's rights. She then became the first female full professor at Columbia University's law school, where she wrote the first law school casebook on sex discrimination.

In 1972 she co-founded The Women's Rights Project at the American Civil Liberties Union and participated in over 300 cases of gender discrimination by 1974, arguing six discrimination cases before the Supreme Court, winning five of them. Today, RBG is credited with ending sex discrimination within the law. In 2010, American journalist Dahlia Lithwick wrote in Slate.com that we "owe a debt of thanks directly to Ruth Bader Ginsburg who almost single-handedly convinced the courts and the legislatures to do away with gender classifications."

RBG has become a figure of the Fourth Wave as well as the second. Her fiery oratory skills, no-nonsense approach to discrimination and her widely admired (and unusual) egalitarian marriage have proved inspirational to a younger generation in awe of the hurdles she crossed. In 2015 a tumblr account was created in dedication, which eventually became a book called *Notorious RBG*, a fitting tribute.

women will have true equality when men share the responsibility of bringing up the next generation

Ruth Bader Ginsburg
Quotation from an interview with The Record *in 2001*

NAWAL EL SAADAWI

Sexual rights revolutionary
Egypt; 1931–

Nawal El Saadawi was six years old when she experienced female genital mutilation (FGM). She was shocked and horrified that her otherwise progressive parents could do that to her, and she would spend the rest of her life fighting for the political and sexual rights of Egyptian women.

El Saadawi became a doctor. In this role, she began to make a link between women's physical and psychological problems and political and religious oppression. In 1972, she published the hugely controversial *Women and Sex*, a feminist criticism of FGM and the broader abuses of women's bodies and sexuality as a means of oppression in Egypt. As a result, El Saadawi lost her job as Director at the Ministry of Public Health and a campaign against her and her revolutionary ideas by the Egyptian authorities began.

El Saadawi continued to research the relationship between women, their health and their political landscape. While studying women and neurosis, a prison doctor introduced her to the story of a female death row inmate at one of Egypt's most infamous prisons, who had killed a man and had been sentenced to hanging. This became the narrative of her novel *Woman at Point Zero*. Egyptian publishers rejected the book and it was first published in Lebanon in 1975. It has since been translated into 22 languages.

Things took a more severe turn in the 1980s when El Saadawi helped published a feminist magazine, *Confrontation*. She found herself in prison for three months where she wrote another book, *Memoirs from the Women's Prison*, in eyeliner on toilet paper. In the early 1990s the authorities banned the Arab Women's Solidarity Association that El Saadawi had founded, and she was placed on a death list, fleeing to the U.S., and not returning to Egypt until 1996.

Feminist, dissident, writer, Saadawi has been called Egypt's Simone de Beauvoir. High praise indeed, but El Saadawi is truly exceptional and her battleground was a very different one from de Beauvoir's 1940s Paris. El Saadawi has risked her freedom and her life for the rights of women in one of the most patriarchal cultures in the world. As she once wrote, "Danger has been a part of my life ever since I picked up a pen and wrote. Nothing is more perilous than truth in a world that lies."

my three husbands
were afraid of me,
i am a very
powerful woman

Nawal El Saadawi

MARSHA P JOHNSON AND SYLVIA RIVERA

Foremothers of the trans rights movement
USA; 1945–1992 and 1951–2002

The story of Marsha P Johnson and Sylvia Rivera is one of pioneering heroics and utter tragedy.

Together they spearheaded the New York LGBT movement and were among the first to demand transgender rights. Marsha P Johnson was a flamboyant, popular figure, photographed by Andy Warhol, and was called the "Rosa Parks" of the transgender movement.

The self-identifying drag queens met in Christopher Street, in New York's West Village, the heart of the city's gay scene in the 1970s. Both were present at the Stonewall Inn on the night of the uprising, or what many activists have dubbed "revolution." As the police raided the bar and allegedly set it on fire, Rivera and Johnson fought back, becoming legends in a landmark event in the history of gay rights. In the aftermath, they became founding members of the Gay Liberation Front, as well as together launching STAR—Street Transvestite Action Revolutionaries—renting a home to house trans sex workers and homeless LGBT youth.

In 1973, they were banned for participating in Gay Pride by the LGBT community who said they were giving them "a bad name." Defiantly, Rivera made her way to the stage and condemned the hostile crowd in a truly brilliant speech. Of the tenants she was supporting she said they "do not write women, do not write men, they write STAR." Rivera was pioneering a non-binary gender identity.

In 1992, Johnson was found dead in the Hudson River. The authorities claimed it was suicide but campaigners have suggested it was murder. Rivera died in 2002 of cancer, after years of alcoholism and homelessness; however, in the last few years of life she became sober and returned to activism.

We are still witnessing the murder of black trans women, which can help put into perspective the courage of Johnson and Sylvia to live the lives they did. Unsurprisingly, their stories are little known, having been dismissed by a society that discriminated against them, their histories discarded like Marsha's body in the Hudson. But now, in the light of a renewed fight for transgender rights, Marsha and Sylvia are beginning to be remembered and celebrated for the incredible lives they lived, full of bravery and the fight for equality—even in the face of huge hardships.

74   2
UkP
Una Kroll

UNA KROLL

Rebellious priest
UK; 1925–2017

"We asked for bread and you have given us stone."

This is what Una Kroll famously shouted down from the gallery at the Church of England's General Synod in 1978, and this is what began a lifelong journey to women's ordination.

Perhaps Kroll was born with a rebellious streak—both her parents were spies and she was born out of wedlock. As a young nun she fell in love with and married an American monk, leading to them both being ostracized by their orders. In 1974, Kroll stood for Parliament as an independent on an equal opportunities platform. She showed herself to be rebellious, independent and feminist—qualities not always associated with women and the Church of England.

Kroll said she was "called to be a priest" at just 19 but said she didn't understand that call because women were prevented from being priests at that time. Instead, she studied at Cambridge and became a doctor:

> At 40 the call came back very, very strongly. A lot the women I was treating were discriminated against, and I didn't have a voice either, and I wanted to say something. And that's how I started working as a Christian feminist, a very sincere Christian feminist, it took many years of my life.

In 1997, Kroll became a priest when the Church of Wales—of which she was then a part—began to ordain women. In 2008, Kroll shocked the Church again; she became a Catholic, she said out of solidarity with the women in the Catholic Church who were still being denied priesthood.

Aged 86, she published her autobiography. Speaking to the BBC she explained how she had found the experience difficult and painful because "I was going against the male hierarchy—I was not used to that. I was a very typical middle-class woman who promised to obey her husband. You can imagine how difficult it was for me to speak."

Fictional Feminists

1. Jane Eyre
"I am no bird, and no net ensnares me: I am a free human being with an independent will."
One of feminist trailblazer Charlotte Brontë's most loved characters, Jane Eyre is headstrong, independent and fiery.

2. Rey
When J J Abrams released a new set of *Star Wars* movies in 2016, the world got Rey. Rey is quick-witted, tough, brave and honest. She's kind but daring. And she's the hero that little girls need, to know that they can use light sabers and fly Millennium Falcons, too.

3. Leslie Knope
A small-town bureaucrat with a big passion for women's rights, Leslie Knope in NBC sitcom *Parks and Recreation* is a brilliantly endearing modern feminist challenging everyday sexism.

4. Lisa Simpson
She's smart, she's political, she's a champion of equality and she's a maverick. Lisa Simpson is the feminist voice in one of the world's most popular TV shows.

5. Wonder Woman

Superheroes are women, too, and here's the proof. In her many guises, from comic book to 2017 blockbuster, Wonder Woman has been inspiring girls for generations.

6. Elizabeth Bennet

Stubborn, independent, smart and proud, *Pride and Prejudice's* Lizzy refuses to adhere to society's conventions or to be blinded by wealth and position.

7. Miranda Hobbes

In a pioneering show that saw women talk about sex, *Sex and the City*, Miranda's feminist credentials kept going; educated, successful, working mother and breadwinner.

8. Buffy the Vampire Slayer

Buffy the Vampire Slayer kicked ass. Literally. She unapologetically killed monsters and was unapologetically attractive and sexual. Buffy was always in charge, always saving the day.

9. Mulan

Described as "hardcore and progressive," this is not your average Disney princess. She kills a lot of people to gain her own honor and respect, radically subverting gender roles.

10. Storm

From the world of Marvel Comics came Storm, descendant of an ancient line of African priestesses, all of whom have white hair, blue eyes and the potential to wield magic.

Inspirational Creatives

1. **Virginia Woolf**

   Woolf didn't just help create literary modernism; she power-fully and poignantly articulated the experience of being a woman in a world that discriminated against them.

2. **Margaret Atwood**

   The Canadian's dystopian fantasy novels have become feminist classics. Today, *The Handmaid's Tale* (1985) has been rediscov-ered as a parable used by contemporary feminists to warn against the Trump administration.

3. **Maya Angelou**

   Maya Angelou's poetry celebrated black womanhood and she gave a powerful, poetic voice to the civil rights movement.

4. **Leslee Udwin**

   In 2015, Leslee Udwin directed *India's Daughter*, a documentary about the Delhi gang rape and murder of a 23-year-old student. The film was banned in India, but became a viral hit elsewhere in the world, shining an important light on the country's culture of sexual violence.

5. Jane Austen

Austen's exploration of a woman's choice and agency smartly tells the story of women in the 18th century, but with insight that means her books are still read by millions today.

6. Nora Ephron

"Be the heroine of your own life," she famously wrote. Known as a great rom com writer, Ephron was also a sharp-witted feminist essayist who urged women to go out and live.

7. Jung Chang

Wild Swans tells the story of three generations of Chinese women, as well as the story of the reality of living under Chairman Mao. By writing what became an international bestseller, Chang gave a voice to the most powerless.

8. Sylvia Plath

From *The Bell Jar* to *Ariel*, Plath's articulation of a misogynistic world and her internalization of that experience has seen Plath revered as one of the great feminist literary voices.

9. Ava DuVernay

Film director, screenwriter and activist, Ava DuVernay became the first black woman to be nominated for Best Director at the Oscars for *Selma* (2015).

10. Toni Morrison

In 1998, Toni Morrison won the Nobel Prize in Literature for *Beloved*—a postmodern triumph that explores the language and experiences of black women in the face of oppression.

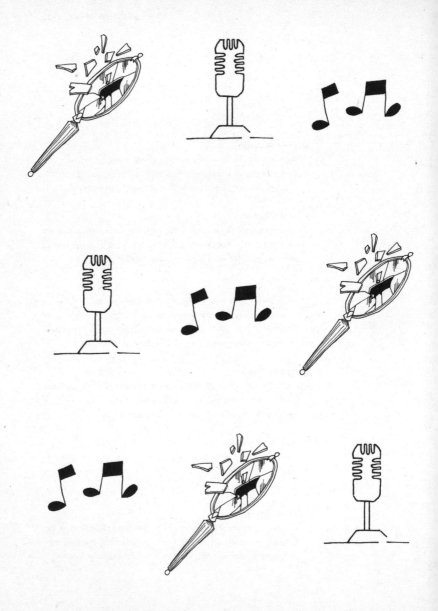

The
Third
Wave

Introducing:
The Third Wave

Feminism's Third Wave came largely from a group of women who rejected grand narratives, neat categorization and a singular notion of what feminism should do and how it should look, and yet believed there still existed the need for a feminist movement.

The women of the Third Wave refused to accept that the 1980s and 1990s were a post-feminist age in which all the demands of the Second Wavers had been adequately met, ushering in a utopia of equality. They recognized that violence against women, sexual harassment, slut shaming, victim blaming and chronic double standards, among many things, were still regular parts of the lives of millions of women—even if women were now in the workplace like never before. As Rebecca Walker wrote in 1992: "the fight is far from over."

As daughters of the Second Wavers, the women of the Third Wave were some of the most empowered and independent in the world. They were born with all the hopes and opportunities their mothers had fought for: they were the first generation in which domesticity, male dominance, discrimination and sexual assault were not simply unavoidable realities for women. But while they recognized their mother's achievements, they were quick to see that the feminist revolution of the 1970s was far from perfect.

The Third Wavers looked for an intersectional approach to women's struggles, focusing on issues of race and sexual orientation. The Third Wave wanted a loud chatter of different, conflicting voices, not the unified chorus of the Second Wave. They explored and expressed feminism through popular culture, not the academia of the 1960s and 70s, believing feminism should be accessible, creative and everyday, not only found in dense tomes on dusty library shelves. They embraced a way of being, and even dressing and wearing make-up, that stood at odds with their foremothers. They fully embraced the idea that feminism could be defined on each individual's terms, that feminism was personal, that feminism could be whatever made women feel empowered—from the DIY zines and punks writing "slut" on their stomachs, to Madonna's overt sexuality or wearing high heels. The Third Wavers celebrated the idea that women can be many, often contradictory, things.

This chapter focuses on American women, with a few British exceptions. That's not to say that feminist women (and men) born from the mid-sixties to the early seventies—the typical Third Waver demographic—didn't exist in the rest of the world. But in the confines of this book's limited space, I wanted to focus on women who identified as part of the Third Wave—those who were actively shaping the movement. Here you'll find the journalists, creatives, writers and thinkers who were purposefully helping to resurrect the feminism movement when many others had thought it redundant.

Another reason for the American dominance of the Third Wave was that a chief vehicle driving it was pop culture—be it the punk of the Riot Grrrl zines, magazines like *Bitch* and *Bust* that contradicted the artificiality and reductive nature of *Vogue* and *Glamour*, or the arrival of TV shows like *Buffy the Vampire Slayer* offering a new type of feminist hero. America has always been the global hub of youth culture, from the birth of the teenager to today's Kardashian empire. In the 1980s and 90s, youth culture was used as a creative, provocative, subversive mouthpiece to remind the world that feminism was not only still relevant, but it was black, it was queer, it was sexual, it was loud, and it was self-defining. And it wasn't going anywhere.

REBECCA WALKER

Original Third Waver
USA; 1969–

For many, Rebecca Walker's 1992 essay, "Becoming the Third Wave," in *Ms. Magazine*, the magazine launched by Second Wave stalwarts Gloria Steinem (page 86) and Dorothy Pitman Hughes, marks the beginning of the often overlooked and more ambiguous Third Wave of feminism.

In the article, 22-year-old Walker, daughter of another Second Wave luminary, author and poet Alice Walker (page 98), relays her anger at the fact that Anita Hill, a law professor, lost her sexual harassment case against Clarence Thomas, a judge who was about to be sworn into the Supreme Court. In the article, Walker launches a rallying cry against the contemporary post-feminist complacency: "I write this as a plea to all women, especially the women of my generation: Let Thomas' confirmation serve to remind you, as it did me, that the fight is far from over."

By rejecting post-feminism and the suggestion that feminism was unnecessary and "finished" in the aftermath of the Second Wave, Walker helped to reignite the movement. After the article, she launched the Third Wave Foundation, with influential authors Jennifer Baumgardner and Amy Richards. The foundation still exists today as the Third Wave Fund—a youth-led gender justice group, which works with young women of color as well as queer, intersex and trans people to help mobilize campaigns and activism.

i am not a postfeminist feminist. i am the third wave

Rebecca Walker
Quotation from the essay "Becoming the Third Wave" written for Ms. magazine

KIMBERLÉ CRENSHAW

Female defender
USA; 1959–

Kimberlé Crenshaw is the first person to say that "intersectionality" is nothing new. As far back as Sojourner Truth (page 39), we have seen women of color understand the unique and multi-faceted nature of their oppression. But it was in the 1980s that Crenshaw coined the term and intersectional theory was recognized as a critical approach to defining structures of discrimination.

Crenshaw, a lawyer, first used the term in a lecture she gave during the 1989 University of Chicago Legal Forum. Crenshaw gave examples of the ways in which the law failed women of color, because either it offered protection against gender discrimination or from racial discrimination, but it did not recognize how those types of oppression interact. She specifically mentioned the case of *DeGraffenreid v General Motors*, in which five black women sued GM on the grounds of race and gender discrimination. They lost the case because the court ruled they'd be giving the plaintiffs "special treatment" and that they'd open up a Pandora's box of discrimination claims.

The gap that these women fell through proved that the oppression and discrimination of intersections were being at best misunderstood and at worst ignored.

Crenshaw was also part of the legal team supporting Anita Hill (page 130). In this infamous case, she felt that Hill became voiceless. Clarence Thomas' defense was built on race, whereas Hill was supported by white feminists (the case was later seen as a watershed moment for workplace sexual harassment), but during that time the specific experience of the black woman was forgotten.

Intersectionality not only sought to define Third Wave feminism, unlocking a key component the Second Wave has often been accused of overlooking, but would go on to become a key tenet of the Fourth Wave movement. In 2015, Crenshaw became an advocate of the #sayhername campaign, seeking to raise awareness around how black women are disproportionately affected by fatal acts of racial injustice.

if we aren't intersectional,
some of us, the most
vulnerable, are going
to fall through
the cracks

Kimberlé Crenshaw
Quotation from an article written for Feminist.com

58   3

Oprah
Winfrey

OPRAH WINFREY

Every woman's Everywoman
USA; 1954–

When Oprah Winfrey first auditioned to become a TV talk show host, she reportedly thought she was "too fat and too black" to be on TV. Just over 30 years later, she is the closest thing America has to royalty (a theory partially proven by how she is often simply referred to by her first name).

Oprah Gail Winfrey, born in 1954 to a poverty-stricken single teenage mother in Mississippi, transformed the American media landscape—and women of colors' place on that horizon. She made a TV show for women one of the most watched TV programs in history; she completely challenged how society and TV could depict black women, and became one of the world's most influential and wealthiest people.

Alongside this, Oprah's empire grew: she launched a magazine; started a book club; gave Oscar-nominated appearances in films and launched her own TV network. She was the first African-American to become a multi-billionaire. After a visit to South Africa, Oprah founded the Oprah Winfrey Leadership Academy for Girls, which opened in 2007. "Oprahfication" and "the Oprah Effect" were phrases coined by the media to try to articulate her phenomenal impact.

Oprah fundamentally redefined notions around women and women of color. Yes, a black woman could be a TV talk show host—in fact, a black woman could be the most successful TV talk show host of all time. But she also changed notions around middle-American housewives, who were not only worth talking to five days a week but deserved to "live their best lives"—the mantra that Oprah claims was her greatest ambition for her audience. Indeed, by talking about everyday issues, with millions of women every day, Oprah elevated her audience from housewives to a powerful consumer base that other TV shows began to compet for. The popularity of the *Oprah* show put issues once perceived as trivial into the spotlight. From domestic violence to weight loss, racism and relationships, Oprah made the everyday lives and concerns of women count.

the biggest
adventure you
can take is to live
the life of
your dreams

Oprah Winfrey
Quotation from an essay published in the July 2002 issue of O, The Oprah Magazine

JUDITH BUTLER

Gender troubler
USA; 1956–

In 1990, Judith Butler published *Gender Trouble: Feminism and the Subversion of Identity* and in 1993 she published *Bodies That Matter: On the Discursive Limits of Sex*. These books offered radical new ways of thinking about gender, and went on to sell all over the world.

Butler argued that gender is performative, or, in other words, gender is not who you are, but what you do. Butler suggested that through continually repeated, stylized actions, society had created the idea of gender that we practice. Her ideas were rooted in philosophy; drawing from Foucault, Freud, de Beauvoir, Lévi-Strauss, Lacan, Irigaray, Wittig, Kristeva.

Although Butler was often criticized for her dense, impenetrable writing style, the ideas themselves were clear. Butler's writings were heavily influential in the emergence of queer theory, drawing from feminist texts, and exploring what impact a new understanding of gender has on sexual identities and sex acts, as well as bringing an intellectual framework to the activism of the LGBT community already taking place.

Butler's writings fundamentally shifted the debate: if, in the Second Wave, the fight had been for womanhood, Butler was asking what womanhood actually is, and who decides.

Today Butler is a professor at the University of California, Berkeley. When Butler published these books, they were visionary in the world of academia. Thirty years later, their influence can be felt from all corners of mainstream life. Dubbed "the gender fluid generation," young people today have a much more non-binary approach to gender and refuse to be confined by identity. Butler's lasting shadow can be seen in society's changing ideas.

masculine and feminine
roles are not
biologically
fixed but
socially
constructed

Judith Butler

EVE ENSLER

Got women talking about vaginas
USA; 1953

Eve Ensler didn't set out to write about vaginas, but after a conversation with a girlfriend, the struggling young playwright realized that the stories of women's vaginas—sex, birthing, relationships, periods, rape—were the stories of women, and those stories needed to be told. And so, *The Vagina Monologues* was born.

The play, which Gloria Steinem describes as "intimate narratives … gathered from more than two hundred interviews and then turned into poetry for the theatre," was originally performed by Ensler in 1996, and was an instant hit. Since then, it has been translated into 48 languages, been performed in 140 countries and ran for over a decade in England, Mexico and France.

As a result of *The Vagina Monologues* and women sharing their stories with her, Ensler became increasingly aware of sexual violence around the world. And so, on February 14, 1998, she launched V-day (with "V" standing for vaginas, Valentines and victory) as an international day of solidarity. Each year, charity performances of *The Vagina Monologues* take place and Ensler has spent time in countries such as Afghanistan, the Democratic Republic of Congo, Kenya and Iraq meeting with and talking to victims of sexual violence. In 2012, the movement became One Billion Rising and has now raised over $100 million for education, safe houses and community-based anti-violence programs across the globe.

In 2011, the *Guardian* named her one of the 100 most influential women in the world, claiming, "Ensler is a uniquely inspirational woman. No one can resist her when they hear her speak."

one of the most
radical things
women can do
is to love their bodies

Eve Ensler

ANITA HILL

Spokeswoman
USA; 1956–

On October 11, 1991, 35-year-old Anita Hill testified against her boss, Clarence Thomas, who had been recently nominated by President Bush to be a Supreme Court judge. Anita Hill's testimony provoked three major things. First, political theatre and a media circus as a three-day testimony was televised. Second, it became a watershed moment in understanding workplace sexual harassment. And thirdly, the injustice of the case mobilized many women to run for public office (and win), leading the media to dub 1992 as "the Year of the Woman."

Hill, a law professor, had worked with Thomas when he was the head of the Equal Employment Opportunity Commission. When Thomas asked Hill out on a date and she refused, he began to repeatedly press her on why. When they were alone, he began "to use work conversations to discuss sex ... His conversations were very vivid."

Clarence denied all Hill's allegations. He famously called the case "a high-tech lynching for uppity blacks." Despite the fact that other women came forward with allegations of sexual harassment, Clarence was cleared and successfully became a Supreme Court judge.

Hill's bravery sent an impactful message to the millions of women watching her on TV. Her testimony gave a voice to the reality of workplace harassment, and her description of how she felt about what had happened to her gave other women a language in which to express their own experiences.

Hill's experience was also an example of how a woman of color faced oppression on two fronts: not only was she a victim of sexual harassment, but by Thomas's use of racism as defense, as a black man he managed to eclipse the fact that Hill was a black woman. The intersection of her oppression was entirely overlooked.

Hill might have lost her case but she inspired thousands and arguably began a new era, one in which women began to acknowledge and question sexual harassment in the workplace. And as we have learned, Rebecca Walker used her anger in watching Hill's case to fuel her creation of the Third Wave.

Anita Hill was a name that became relevant again in 2017, in the light of the Harvey Weinstein revelations. As many women came forward about the Hollywood producer's sexual harassment and predatory behavior, actor Alyssa Milano started a Twitter campaign called #metoo, encouraging other women to share their experiences. Thousands responded, and the pioneering efforts of Anita Hill were remembered once more.

34   3
Ab
Alison
Bechdel

ALISON BECHDEL

Feminist film critic
USA; 1960–

Alison Bechdel admits the Bechdel Test came about accidentally, claiming she "stole" the idea from a friend, Liz Wallace, and put it in her comic strip, *Dykes to Watch Out For*, in 1985. The strip ran from 1983 to 2008, and was one of the first long-running depictions of lesbian lives.

Bechdel's cartoon depicts two women having a conversation about going to the cinema. One of the women says she'll only go if the film satisfies three criteria: it has to have at least two women in it, they have to talk to each other, and they have to talk about something other than a man. The Bechdel Test, as it became known, is applied now all over the world and has become a useful tool to articulate the insidious sexism in the film industry.

Historians have since pointed out that Virginia Woolf made a similar point in her 1929 essay, "A Room of One's Own." She wrote:

> [...] almost without exception they are shown in their relation to men. It was strange to think that all the great women of fiction were, until Jane Austen's day, not only seen by the other sex, but seen only in relation to the other sex. And how small a part of a woman's life is that.

In 2006, Bechdel published *Fun Home*, a graphic novel that tells the story of Bechdel discovering her own sexuality, her relationship with her gay father and his death. The novel was turned into a Broadway play in 2015, won five Tony Awards and became the first Broadway show with a lesbian protagonist.

NAOMI WOLF

Challenger to beauty
USA; 1962–

"'Beauty' is a currency system like the gold standard. Like any economy, it is determined by politics, and in the modern age in the West it is the last, best belief system that keeps male dominance intact."

In 1990, at just 28, Naomi Wolf published *The Beauty Myth*. It was a bestseller and Wolf became another powerful voice challenging the notion of post-feminism.

Her short book is akin to a controlled explosion: via thorough research into the lives of American women, peppered with academic references, Wolf sets out her argument breathlessly and urgently, systematically pulling apart the beauty industry and revealing how its very design seeks to objectify, commodify and undermine a newly empowered generation of women.

For Wolf, the boom of beauty products, fitness regimes, weight-loss plans, and the increasing pornification of mainstream media, culture and advertising was a reaction to the successfully liberated women of the 1970s and the subsequent women who now existed in offices—and in power—across the country. Wolf writes, "We are in the midst of a violent backlash against feminism that uses images of female beauty as a political weapon against women's advancement: the beauty myth."

Wolf believes that the industry and its narrow, highly sexualized notion of "beauty" replaced the shackles of domesticity that the Second Wavers had thrown off, in order to try to undo women's newfound political, social and sexual liberation. Thanks to the booming beauty industry of the 1980s, women literally had to spend more time and money looking eternally youthful and slim to compete in the new world they'd only just been allowed into. This multi-billion-dollar industry ensured that a woman's worth was tied directly to how she looked. Men decided what was beautiful and women paid for it—in more ways than one.

a culture fixated on female thinness is not an obsession about female beauty, but an obsession about female obedience

Naomi Wolf
Quotation from The Beauty Myth

AMY RICHARDS AND
JENNIFER BAUMGARDNER

Rebel authors
USA; 1971–, 1970–

It's not surprising that Amy Richards and Jennifer Baumgardner wrote one of the key texts of the Third Wave when you learn they met at *Ms. Magazine* and their boss was Gloria Steinem.

As two young women in New York in the early 1990s, the pair wanted to record the phase of feminism they were witnessing. In their book *Manifesta*, they discuss both the backdrop of their fore-mothers' struggles for freedom and their own generation being the first to take advantage of those hard-fought battles, to the development of a new feminist identity that was pushing at the barriers of what feminism could be and what feminists could look like—a feminism not explored through the political but through the personal and the cultural.

In particular, Richards and Baumgardner used popular culture to explore how this new feminism was manifesting, from Madonna and *Buffy the Vampire Slayer* to magazines like *Bitch* and *Bust*, and books like *Bitch: In Praise of Difficult Women* by Elizabeth Wurtzel. They also championed the arrival of "the girlie culture," which they define as the "intersection of feminism with feminine culture." The women wrote that "Girlie encompasses the tabooed symbols of women's feminine enculturation—Barbie dolls, make-up, fashion magazines, high heels—and says using them isn't shorthand for 'we've been duped.'"

Their book not only helped kick-start a conversation for thousands of women but also articulated the social and cultural faces of the movement. In a sea of zines and fringe bands, *Manifesta* was key in defining the Third Wave—and, to the outside at least, legitimizing it as a movement.

Prior to writing the book, the women had been activists. In 1997, along with Rebecca Walker, Richards and Baumgardner founded the Third Wave Foundation, a group dedicated to supporting those working toward "gender, racial, economic and social justice".

KATHLEEN HANNA

Subversive punk-rocker
USA; 1968–

Kathleen Hanna was the lead singer of Bikini Kill—the band at the heart of the 1990s punk Riot Grrrl movement. Not only did she lead a punk subculture that promoted the voice of young women, she also became one of the leaders of the Third Wave, putting a feminist agenda at the heart of everything she did, as both a musician and an activist.

Hanna was a subversive, challenging new voice. She wrote "slut" on her stomach and she had a strict "girls at the front" policy, inviting girls to the front of the mosh pit. She even physically removed men from the audience who were heckling her—all while performing anthems that gave solidarity and hope to, in her own words, teenage girls who felt that they were "weirdos."

Hanna's lyrics, and her zines, including the *Bikini Kill Zine*, which published the Riot Grrrl manifesto, attempted to address "feminist issues through a punk rock lens" and tackled violence against women, sexual assault, empowerment, sexuality and identity, as well as more practical concerns such as safety in the mosh pit.

Since the band split in 1997, Hanna has been an outspoken advocate for Planned Parenthood.

"I just wanted to make sure other girls found out about feminism. It didn't have to be our mums' feminism; we needed to build on what they had created and change it and make it better."

Kathleen Hanna
(from the article "What Happens When a Riot Grrrl Grows Up?"
published in the *Guardian* in 2014)

i would rather be the
obnoxious feminist
girl than complicit
in my own
dehumanization

Kathleen Hanna

OSEZ LE FÉMINISME!

Founded 2009

Translated as Dare to be Feminist!, Osez le Féminisme! is a French collective that was founded in 2009 in response to funding cuts to public family-planning services. What started as a group of a dozen activists from various political organizations came together to create a united front that now has 26 groups across France and a Facebook community of 10,000.

The group have launched campaigns that have garnered international attention, such as the 2014 Take Back the Metro, to combat the high rate of sexual harassment and assault that was taking place on France's public transport. The women plastered posters around the Metro that offered advice on what to do if assaulted, as well as a reminder to men not to "manspread." One poster read "It is preferable to keep your legs together. Testicles are not made of crystal and will not explode. You can thus leave more space for your neighbours. You will no longer inflict this visual pollution on them." In 2017, they protested against the showcasing of a retrospective of the work of alleged rapist Roman Polanski and in the 2017 elections, the group, along with other organizations, worked together to block the National Front candidate.

The group's ethos is "Feminism is not a women's fight." It's a social struggle that extends to issues including abortion, maternity rights, femicide, rape and parental care, as well as working to end discrimination against the LGBT community.

RIOT GRRRL

Riotous punk group
USA; 1990s

Riot Grrrl, the feminist punk movement born in the early 1990s in Washington state, was the perfect storm of time and place.

The 1970s and 1980s saw the success of female punk singers—such as Siouxsie Sioux and Patti Smith—and yet punk itself was often rife with misogyny, with women at gigs nicknamed

"I believe with my wholeheartmindbody that girls constitute a revolutionary soul force that can, and will change the world for real." (from the Riot Grrl manifesto, written in 1990)

Riot Grrrl

"coathangers," as they were expected to stand holding their boyfriend's coat. Riot Grrrl was a reaction to this, as well as a way for young women to express their feelings at the sexism they faced in a supposedly post-feminist world. And in the world of Riot Grrrl, young women had more power than they realized.

Defined by a feminist agenda and expressed through music, zines and a DIY philosophy, bands Bikini Kill and Bratmobile were at the heart of the movement. Allegedly, Bratmobile member Jen Smith used the phase "riot girl" in a letter to bandmate Allison Wolfe, to reflect the growing feminist mood. Wolfe then collaborated with Kathleen Hanna (page 135) of Bikini Kill on a zine and called it Riot Grrrl—adding the extra "r"s to angrily reclaim the word.

Riot Grrrl bands and zines encouraged women to have a voice in the male world of punk and beyond. On and off stage, they tackled issues of rape, domestic violence, sexuality, female empowerment and slut shaming. It was also a form of consciousness raising, with collectives encouraging women to meet and share their experiences.

The movement has been criticized for being made up of almost exclusively white women and ignoring the experiences of women of color. But Riot Grrrl must also be remembered for what they did achieve, namely igniting a feminist movement that listened to the needs of young women.

94   3
Gu
Guerrilla Girls

GUERRILLA GIRLS

Artistic activists
Unknown; founded 1985

In 1985, seven radical feminists decided to challenge the sexism and racism they saw ingrained in the art world. The trigger was an exhibition at New York's prestigious MoMA (Museum of Modern Art) called "An International Survey of Recent Painting and Sculpture," which only featured 13 women out of the 165 artists listed. The protesters decided to be anonymous, wearing gorilla masks in public, claiming "Our anonymity keeps the focus on the issues, and away from who we might be."

The group called out the lack of diversity in major art institutions using posters, stickers and street projects, as well as criticizing male artists who showed support for those institutions. "Do you have to be naked to get into the Met?" they famously asked, referring to the fact that there were minimal female artists but plenty of naked female bodies in the gallery.

Since then, the Guerrilla Girls (55 people have been members for varying lengths of time) have taken their feminist art activism to countries around the world, with major retrospectives of their work in Spain and the U.S. Today they are still protesting against sexism, racism, Donald Trump and working conditions for art gallery employees, with one giant poster in America reading, "Dear Art Gallery: Selling art is so expensive! No wonder you can't pay all your employees a living wage!"

Their activism is subversive and humorous, and their message was, and continues to be, bold, uncomfortable, provocative and uncompromising. The rebellious, playful and daring spirit of the Guerrilla Girls can be seen in the Riot Grrrl movement (page 138) that was to follow and, similarly, both parties reject the notion of individual leadership, preferring to celebrate their collective efforts, something that became a recurring theme of the Third Wave.

68 3
Sg
Spice Girls

SPICE GIRLS

Girl power!
UK; formed 1994

What was "Girl Power"? "Friendship that never ends?" A Union Jack dress at the Brit Awards? Or a group of 20-something British women selling millions of records around the world?

When the Spice Girls arrived in 1994, skepticism came with them. Feminists asked if they were an articulation of the Third Wave bubbling over into the mainstream, or whether it was a case of feminism-lite—a commodification of the cooler Grrrl and Girlie culture that young women had organically cultivated.

For some, Girl Power was a legitimate expression of independence, empowerment and female solidarity. Tweens growing up to the song "Wannabe" were wide-eyed at the arrival of an all-girl band who challenged nineties' men's magazine culture, who were louder and more fun than the male-dominated Brit Pop, and who were a mixed bag of different (albeit constructed) personalities which were meant to appeal to us all. In the late nineties, Geri Halliwell began to work with the UN as a goodwill ambassador and with Marie Stopes International, calling for sex education for young people and raising awareness around sexual health.

But more cynically, was the band the revenge of post-feminism? The cruel, mocking proof that all the fight for equality needed was a peace sign and a cunning PR mogul? Feminists such as Caitlin Moran have criticized the group, accusing the band of eradicating feminism, claiming their message was hollow. In 2011, she told the *Guardian* of the group, "You're literally going to tell me as a woman that the two things that are good for me are 1) to make me feel I should go back to wearing a very short skirt, and 2) be friends with my girlfriends? And in exchange for that you're basically going to wipe out feminism for a decade? Thanks!"

"Girl Power" was one of the early examples of the corporate world realizing that feminism could sell. But it was also a great slogan for the 10-year-olds who bought their records, and still resonates with many of them as adults today.

BITCH MEDIA

Badass bitches
USA; founded 1996

Out of the back of a station wagon, Lisa Jervis, Benjamin Shaykin and Andi Zeisler began their media empire. It was 1996 and the college graduates had created and published their first zine, called *Bitch*, a space to write intelligently and critically about popular culture—all through a feminist lens. Little did they know that those 300 copies would become an integral voice of the Third Wave.

The magazine's name set the tone: it was the defiant reclaiming of a word that intentionally used language women had previously rejected, separating itself from the Second Wave, and thereby attracting women who would never have picked up a "women's lib" magazine. It was perceived as younger, more outrageous, less earnest and a break with the past. Feminists didn't have to be their bra-burning mothers—they could be sexy, they could wear short skirts, they could use the word "bitch."

Bitch quickly grew from a hand-stapled zine to a color magazine with offices and staff. Today, Bitch Media is a not-for-profit organization that also works with schools and communities on understanding feminist conversations, as well as hosting a community library.

The original founders claim the magazine is as necessary to today as it was in the mid-nineties. This may or may not be true, but it's still important to consider the impact it had on the Third Wave. *Bitch* was key in formulating conversations such as: How do I identify? And who gets to decide? It was part of the beginning of a new era in which feminism was not a rule book, there were no grand narratives, but instead a multi-faceted, contradictory, provocative mix of identities and opinions—from a critical analysis of *Beverly Hills 90210* and the Spice Girls to interviews with bell hooks, Guerrilla Girls and cartoonist Lynda Barry.

Political Leaders

1. Elizabeth Warren

A tireless voice that defends Americans' right to family planning; who won't be bullied by her male opponents; and who, after being told to be quiet, continued to voice her discontent. It was of Warren that Mitch McConnell said, "Nevertheless, she persisted."

2. Victoria Woodhull

A leader of the American suffrage movement, Woodhull also ran for president in 1872.

3. Hillary Rodham Clinton

From her electrifying speech at Wellesley College that saw her on the cover of *Time*, to her famous declaration that "Human rights are women's rights," and eventually making history as the first female presidential candidate for a major party, Clinton is a lifelong champion of the rights of women and girls and a feminist icon the world over.

4. Harriet Harman

The longest-serving British female Member of Parliament (MP), Harriet Harman is a hero. Not only was she a pioneering MP who created the Labour Women's Parliamentary Party but she pushed through legislation that aimed to make women's lives better—both inside and outside the House of Commons.

5. Barbara Castle

When the Dagenham sewing machinists walked out on strike in 1969 against unequal pay it was Labour MP Barbara Castle who came to their aid. Intervening and ending the strike, she saw the women received 92 percent of what the men do and as a result pushed through the Equal Pay Act of 1970.

6. Eva Perón

Perón was credited with getting Argentine women the vote in 1946. She also created the country's first large feminist organization that brought thousands of women into politics for the very first time.

7. Michelle Obama

"When they go low, we go high!" Michelle Obama, the first black First Lady, was known for her work with girls and education and her incredible oratory skills. Ahead of the 2015 election, Michelle Obama gave electrifying speeches that inspired women the world over.

8. Julia Gillard

The former Australian Prime Minister caught the world's attention when she spectacularly took the leader to task for his misogyny. The speech racked up millions of views on YouTube and Gillard became a feminist hero.

9. Benazir Bhutto

Bhutto was the first woman to head a democratic government in a Muslim majority nation. While she was pro-life and permitted fundamentalist laws that restricted women's rights, she introduced women judges, a woman's bank and all-women police stations.

10. Michelle Bachelet

The first female president of Chile (and first female defense secretary), Bachelet is a fierce advocate for gender equality. In 2017, under her leadership, Chile saw a landmark bill legislating abortion in some circumstances.

11. Vigdís Finnbogadóttir

The world's first democratically elected female president, as President of Iceland, Finnbogadóttir worked to promote girls' education and had the motto "Never let the women down."

12. Angela Merkel

She won't call herself a feminist, but as one of the most powerful women in the world, she is an international symbol of female achievement and political power.

13. Viscountess Nancy Astor

American-born Nancy Astor was the first female Member of Parliament to take her seat in 1919.

14. Eleanor Roosevelt

"Well-behaved women rarely make history," the First Lady famously said. Roosevelt championed working women, supported women in poverty, encouraged women to vote, chaired the Presidential Committee on the Status of Women under Kennedy, and campaigned to see more women in political life.

15. Jóhanna Sigurðardóttir

Sigurðarddóttir was Iceland's first female Prime Minister and the world's first openly lesbian head of government.

there is still
so much history
yet to be made

Michelle Obama
Quotation from the Keynote Address at Young African Women Leaders Forum in 2011

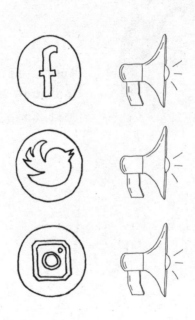

The
Fourth
Wave

Introducing: The Fourth Wave

The precise beginnings and endings of "waves" of feminism are impossible to define. But when it comes to the Fourth Wave, there were three years where you could see a new type of feminism erupt, a fresh shoot of consciousness grow, a moment in time where women rose up and collectively said "enough is enough." Those years were 2011–present.

Caitlin Moran's international bestseller *How to Be a Woman* (2011) was followed by the creation of the Everyday Sexism Project (2012), the first airing of Lena Dunham's *Girls* (2012) and Chimamanda Ngozi Adichie's seminal TED Talk (2012). Feminist writer Rebecca Solnit said 2014 was the year she had been waiting for all her life because it was the year that "private issues" of domestic violence "became public." In that same year, grassroots, action-led groups like Sisters Uncut formed, while Laverne Cox became the first openly transgender person to appear on the cover of *Time*. In those few years, the voices of women grew louder, more urgent and more powerful, creating momentum for change. The following year, Hillary Rodham Clinton announced she was running for President, and, two years later, thousands of women took to the streets in 84 countries across the globe for the 2017 Women's March, the largest protest of its kind.

One of the defining ways by which women found their voice was the internet. Women and girls utilized the arrival of social-media platforms to create communities, launch campaigns and harness a collective power. Hashtags and online petitions became the digital picket line, serving both as a show of solidarity and a message of resistance. Everday sexism began as a Twitter hashtag; the Black Lives Matter movement was started on Facebook by three women; #metoo was used across platforms to highlight the scale of sexual assault. Social media fuelled the Fourth Wave, allowing women to connect and organize, but also to share experiences. And on the internet you could find places where you wouldn't be talked over or dismissed or mocked. On the internet you would be believed. Or, at least by some. Because of course there is another, darker side to life as an outspoken woman online, something many of the women in this chapter know all too well.

But if the internet is their megaphone, what are their issues? Representation in places of power, intersectionality, transgender rights, reproductive rights, violence against women, supporting refugee women, empowerment, giving women tools to sustain economic independence, the adoption of paternity leave and equality in the workplace, sexual assault on college and university campuses, gender fluidity, climate change. These issues weren't new but some were openly discussed for the first time, and all had a rejuvenated urgency to be eradicated or fixed or supported. And this time men were involved, too. Emma Watson launched her HeForShe campaign with the UN (2014)—men were no longer the enemy; they were essential allies, allies who suffered in their own unique ways with the pressure and pitfalls of toxic hyper-masculinity. The Fourth Wave looked for the bigger, structural problems: the enemy is not men, the enemy is privilege.

And the word itself was resurrected. Brushed aside in the 1990s and early 2000s, feminism had for many become a byword for man-hating, bra-burning militants. The Fourth Wave disman-tled that myth once and for all; the Fourth Wave made feminism necessary again—important, but also fallible, multi-faceted, more inclusive. And soon it became cool, a part of the main-stream, before it eventually became profitable, a bandwagon that a washing-up liquid brand jumped on. Older feminists complained of the individualistic, self-centered nature of modern feminism, where personal economic success and the promotion of brand "me" was mistakenly labelled as a feminist act, the opposite of a movement that began as a collective political endeavor to achieve equality for all.

It's hard to determine the success of the Fourth Wave—partly because we're still in it, and partly because while we have more women in positions of power, we have Donald Trump. And while we have more women telling their own stories, mental health problems among teenage girls are higher than ever. There is not, and never has been, a straightforward path for feminism.

As with every chapter I'm keen to acknowledge the women we couldn't fit in, which is no reflection on those women or girls, but more the impossibility to tell this story in a truly 360-degree way within this number of pages. The women I've picked are just a sample of the Fourth Wave movement. From Yemen to China, the UK to Afghanistan and America, the Fourth Wave is reverberating around the world. And why did feminism return with a tidal wave of activity in that moment—seeping into all corners of the globe, at all levels of society, found in so many communities? These things never have a simple answer, but be sure that the internet and social media woke the world up. Women found new ways to be heard, new ways to turn the tide.

The lie that feminism had died, that it was divisive, bitter and unpleasant, had been found out. Inequality was still debilitating, damaging and degrading women, and women still needed feminism. And a whole new generation was going to let the world know.

65   4

Jk

Jude Kelly

JUDE KELLY

Artistic director
UK; 1954–

The Women of the World festival first took place in 2011 to commemorate 100 years of International Women's Day (founded by Clara Zetkin in 1910, page 52) at London's Southbank Centre, and was launched by Jude Kelly, the theatre director and producer-turned-artistic director of the center, the country's largest cultural institution. Six years later, WOW has spread across the world. As stated on the company's website, "20 festivals across five continents to date and over one million women and girls, men and boys taking part. From Finland to Folkestone and Derry to Dhaka, crossing further continents to Harlem and Hargeysa, Brisbane and Baltimore, WOW continues to grow and cross borders around the world." And with every border crossed, Kelly's infectious energy and commitment to social change are abundantly apparent.

The festival discusses all issues that impact women's lives, from an intersectional, international perspective, including workshops for feminist under-tens to panel debates on issues such as transgenderism, alcohol, rape and domestic violence, as well as performances by choirs and comedy sets. WOW is the spirit, soul and heart of the Fourth Wave brought to life over a few days. There's a grassroots energy that encourages discussion, debate and honesty, and the communal experience nods to the consciousness raising groups and safe spaces of feminism's history. With a mix of experts and audience participation, WOW is the real-world platform for feminists to meet, connect and push forward change.

In 2013, Kelly launched BAM—Being a Man festival—an important festival that serves to help reconsider and define modern masculinity, all of which is an essential part of Fourth Wave feminism.

36   4

Am

Anne-Marie
Slaughter

ANNE-MARIE SLAUGHTER

Advocate for working women
USA; 1958–

"Having it all" was a phrase popularized in the 1980s. It described the new influx of middle-class women in the workplace (it's important to remember that working-class women had always been there), particularly in senior management roles, and referred to the contemporary "superwoman," juggling both a career and a family. Think Diane Keaton in the 1987 movie *Baby Boom*.

With time, however, many feminists—especially younger ones—felt this was an unhelpful phrase that created impossible expectations for women. As feminist writer Rebecca Traister put it, "It is a trap, a setup for inevitable feminist short-fall."

This was the crux of Anne-Marie Slaughter's article in *The Atlantic*, published in 2012 and quoted on the following page. Called "Why Women Still Can't Have It All," Slaughter, the first woman Director of Policy Planning at the U.S. State Department, international lawyer and academic, penned the essay after she left her prestigious White House role to spend more time with her family. Once the poster woman for Having It All—big job in Washington, two sons—Slaughter wrote the piece to bust the myth and to make the case that business and culture should fundamentally change, instead of expecting women to do the impossible and then making them feel bad when they can't.

It was one of *The Atlantic*'s most read pieces and Slaughter has gone on to publish two books about being a parent in the workplace and has become an advocate for flexible working. For many, the article was significant in starting a conversation that took the emphasis off women and placed the responsibility back on society.

"It is time for women in leadership positions to recognize that although we are still blazing trails and breaking ceilings, many of us are also reinforcing a falsehood: that 'having it all' is, more than anything, a function of personal determination."

Anne-Marie Slaughter
(from the article "Why Women Still Can't Have It All", published in *The Atlantic* in 2011)

64   4

Rs

Rebecca
Solnit

REBECCA SOLNIT

On-point essayist
USA; 1961–

If you haven't heard of Rebecca Solnit, you've doubtlessly heard the term "mansplaining"—the universally applied and exceptionally useful word that denotes the infuriating, yet common, experience of a man explaining to a woman something she knows all about.

The phrase was born from Solnit's 2008 essay, "Men Explain Things to Me," which the American essayist and author wrote after talking to a man at a party who asked her about her writing. She mentioned her then-recent book about Eadweard Muybridge. "He cut me off soon after I mentioned Muybridge," Solnit writes. "'And have you heard about the *very important* Muybridge book that came out this year?'" Solnit's friend attempts to interrupt three or four times, saying, "That's her book." Finally, the penny drops: "And then, as if in a nineteenth-century novel, he went ashen." The essay went viral and the term "mansplaining" is now in the *Oxford English Dictionary* and common vernacular.

"Men Explain Things to Me" was later published as the lead essay in a book of the same name in 2014—the year that Solnit said she had been "waiting all my life for." Writing in the *Guardian*, Solnit argues that 2014 was the year that so-called "private" issues of violence and sexual violence against women finally became "public." And Solnit's own writings, which date back to 1992, have been rediscovered and used as weapons in the arsenal to break that silence. In 2017, she published *The Mother of All Questions: Further Feminism*, a collection of her previously published writings on feminism, as well as a new essay, *A Short History of Silence*. Solnit's writings are not just insightful and smart but offer a language and framework for women—and men—to make sense of the world. The *New York Times* has called her "the voice of the resistance," offering hope in a Trump age.

SHERYL SANDBERG

Star of Silicon Valley
USA; 1969–

In 2008, Sheryl Sandberg left Google to join Facebook as its Chief Operating Officer. She was one of the very few women in a senior executive role in Silicon Valley and she did what was pretty unthinkable up until that point: she talked about it. Reflecting years later she said, "I grew up in the business world. You never talk about being a woman because someone might notice you are a woman."

Her 15-minute TED Talk at the TEDWomen conference in 2010 was an instant hit and in 2013 she explored those ideas further in her first book, *Lean In*. Not only was it a *New York Times* bestseller for over a year, but *Lean In* became a foundation, launched that year, to help empower women with Lean In Circles where women meet and support one another. It even became part of the vernacular, as a byword for how women can succeed in their careers.

Using research and personal experiences, Sandberg highlighted the confidence gap brought about by a gendered society and argued that women have to lean in, push themselves forward, raise their hands, and, as she said in her original TED Talk, "sit at the table." She also acknowledged unconscious bias and the need for men to be more hands-on in the home.

But Sandberg's type of feminism was not readily accepted by everyone. She spoke primarily of the experience of the white, privileged woman, paying little attention to the reality of single working mothers, women of color or working-class women. She has become synonymous with a modern, neoliberalist brand of feminism that promotes the needs of the individual, with little concern for the collective needs of more vulnerable women. In May 2016, after Sandberg was tragically widowed, she admitted that previously she had not given enough credit to the realities of single motherhood.

78   4
El
Elaine
Welteroth

ELAINE WELTEROTH

Inspiring editor
USA; 1986–

Elaine Welteroth is the editor of *Teen Vogue* and, since the magazine was placed under her direction in 2016, she and her team have not only dramatically increased sales but radically challenged traditional expectations of who young women are and what they want to read.

Appointed to the role of editor at just 29 (becoming Condé Nast's youngest ever editor and only the second African-American editor), Welteroth champions diversity—both in the cover stars she features, the contributors and the topics covered. While still offering standard teenager fare such as spot cover-up and nail polish colors, Welteroth's *Teen Vogue* has political bite, exploring issues such as the Syrian refugee crisis, Standing Rock, gay marriage, having incarcerated parents, Catalan independence and the Trump administration.

Teen Vogue's reinvention is a victory for modern feminism: a young woman of color is running an influential title that has a global reach, and the content of the magazine confirms what many have long dismissed—that young women are engaged, informed and political. Increasing sales figures and website traffic have demonstrated that Welteroth recognized, responded and connected to a hunger for political knowledge and analysis told through a voice that young women can relate to. It is not just a success for Welteroth, it is a success for us all.

12   4
Cm
Caitlin
Moran

CAITLIN MORAN

Honest speaker
UK; 1975–

Caitlin Moran wrote *How to Be a Woman* in five months. Within less than a year of publication in 2011 it had sold 400,000 copies in 16 countries. The *New York Times* called it "a book that needed to be written. No doubt part of its popularity was Moran's unmistakable humor and razor-sharp insight, but it also marked, for many, the resurgence of feminism, and specifically a kind of feminism inspired by Germaine Greer or, in Moran's own words, the book was 'like *The Female Eunuch* but with jokes about my knickers.'"

Embracing a word that, for many, had been reduced to man-hating 1970s academic books, Moran attempted to resurrect not only the F-word but, in turn, women's relationship with themselves and with men. *How to Be a Woman* is confessional, warm and funny; it is hugely relatable and candid, discussing abortion, eating disorders, masturbation, love and body issues. For many, the appeal of Moran's book is that she is just like you, and if she is a feminist that meant you must be a feminist, too. On sold-out book tours across the country, Moran would make the audience stand on a chair and shout "I am a feminist!" Moran's insistence on falling back in love with a word and movement many thought redundant helped propel the Fourth Wave.

Her honesty and her own stories were a personal hook that told a political story—another Second Wave refrain revisited. Through the telling of her own upbringing—one of eight siblings, homeschooled by chaotic parents—Moran brought feminism to a whole new generation of young women and girls, ones who'd never heard of Germaine Greer and ones who never thought they were a feminist.

There has been controversy. Moran has been accused by other feminists, including the current editor of *Bitch* magazine, of a "non-intersectional feminism." In response, Moran has said, "I wrote *How to Be a Woman*, not How to be ALL Women. I would never presume to speak for 3 billion women."

"Do you have a vagina? And do you want to be in charge of it? If you said yes to both, then congratulations! You're a feminist".

Caitlin Moran
(from *How to Be a Woman*)

JESSICA VALENTI

Internet vigilante
USA; 1978–

If the Fourth Wave is predominantly associated with online communities, one of the earliest gathering of online feminists was around Jessica Valenti.

Valenti founded feministing.com in 2004—long before the likes of Caitlin Moran or Chimamanda Ngozi Adichie reclaimed the word—a platform for feminist analysis of everything from pop culture to politics, and to provide support to young feminists to participate in real-world activism. As described by the *Guardian*, Valenti helped define the contemporary nature of the movement and how it structures itself today: "At a time when the death of feminism was being announced, they launched discussions, voices, support and campaigns around the world." She has since published six books, including the *New York Times* bestseller *Sex Object: A Memoir*, and paved the way for a new breed of young feminist voices, pioneering a space online for a new feminism to flourish. In 2011, she was named one of the *Guardian*'s Top 100 Women.

Valenti, however, was one of the first to experience the misogyny that has become part of daily life for women online. In 2016, the *Guardian* revealed she was in their top 10 victims of online abuse that took place within the *Guardian* reader comments section (along with seven other women—three white and four black—and two black men). Valenti's brave new digital world for feminism sparked a revolution but uncovered a sinister resistance.

LAURA BATES

Global feminist voice
UK; 1986–

Laura Bates never set out to be a global feminist voice and a key founder of the Fourth Wave. Instead, she had dreams of becoming an actor. But after a particularly unpleasant week in April 2012, when she'd been groped on the bus and catcalled in the street, Bates set up a small space online, called Everyday Sexism, to share these experiences with other women. Almost immediately hundreds of stories came pouring in. Soon the website and the hashtag had not only become an international platform for women and girls to share their own experiences in a community of solidarity, but it also sent a renewed message of zero tolerance of any form of sexism. Within three years, the site had 100,000 entries from across the globe.

Harnessing the power of the internet and the arrival of social media platforms, Bates revealed the true extent to which women face sexism—from comments made by strangers in the street to rape and assault. She has campaigned on issues such as removing sexually violent content from Facebook and worked with the British Transport Police to combat sexual harassment on public transport. Appearing across the media, in front of the UN and alongside world leaders, Bates is a passionate, powerful voice who works to expose and end the sexism woven into all facets of the lives of women and girls.

Bates spends a lot of time visiting schools and universities across the UK to speak with young men and women to undo the harmful stereotypes they face. In 2014, she published her first book, *Everyday Sexism*, a collection of the stories submitted to the website, and in 2016, she published *Girl Up*, a survival guide for young girls in today's society.

KAREN INGALA SMITH

CEO by day, feminist by night
UK; DOB unknown

Karen Ingala Smith is counting dead women.

She began counting dead women in January 2012 when she noticed that eight women had been killed by their male partners or relatives' partners in just three days. She later wrote, "Perhaps because it was the beginning of the year, I just started counting, and once I'd started, I couldn't stop." Ingala Smith is still counting. In 2016, her website logged 124 dead women murdered by men in the UK.

By day, Ingala Smith is the CEO of nia, a London-based charity working to end violence and sexual violence against women and girls. She is also the co-creator of the Femicide Census with Women's Aid (England), launched in 2016, to collect and analyze information on fatal male violence against women.

Ingala Smith uses Twitter to count—and honor—dead women but also to reinforce the notion that these are both individual incidents and symptomatic of a society in which male violence is permitted and ingrained. Her project is an important and deeply moving reminder of an urgent and still too often overlooked issue.

37   4

CP

Caroline
Criado-Perez

CAROLINE CRIADO-PEREZ

Feminist campaigner
UK; 1984–

Caroline Criado-Perez fights for women to be visible and vocal in public life, even in the face of heinous online abuse.

Criado-Perez's first high-profile feminist campaign was a response to listening to all-male panels on BBC Radio 4 discuss issues directly related to women, such as breast cancer and pregnancy. Feeling frustrated at the lack of representation, in 2012, along with Catherine Smith, she launched The Women's Room, an online database of female experts, in order for it to become inexcusable for the media to exclude women's voices.

The following year, in 2013, when the Bank of England announced it was replacing Elizabeth Fry with Winston Churchill on the £5 note, Criado-Perez launched a campaign to keep a woman on a British bank note (other than the queen), pointing to the 2010 Equality Act, which ensures public institutions commit to eradicating discrimination. Criado-Perez collected 35,000 signatures and later that year the recently appointed head of the Bank of England, Mark Carney, announced that Jane Austen would appear on the new £10 note, which went into circulation in September 2017.

Most recently, Criado-Perez successfully campaigned for a statue of Millicent Fawcett (page 37) to be erected in Parliament

Square—the first statue of a woman in the prestigious Westminster square.

Like many Fourth Wavers, Criado-Perez uses social media to fuel her efforts but she was also subject to vicious and threatening online trolling.

ROXANE GAY

Leading essayist
USA; 1974–

Roxane Gay's collection of essays, *Bad Feminist*, published in 2014, reaffirmed an increasingly prevalent opinion that while feminism needed to be embraced, feminism is problematic. She wrote, "Feminism is flawed because it is a movement powered by people and people are inherently flawed." Gay, therefore, lobbies for and practices a more forgiving and accessible feminism than that which many associate with the more absolutist tone of the academic tomes of the Second Wave.

She writes, "I embrace the label of bad feminist because I am human. I am messy. I am not trying to be an example. I am not trying to be perfect ... I am just trying—trying to support what I believe in, trying to do some good in this world, trying to make some noise with my writing while also being myself; a woman who loves pink and likes to get freaky and sometimes dance her ass off to music she knows, *she knows*, is terrible for women."

Gay's writings—both fiction and non-fiction—had been gaining a following, but 2014's *Bad Feminist* elevated her to a globally recognized feminist voice, speaking on issues of equality, race, sexuality and gender. She's since published *Difficult Women*, a collection of short stories, and *Hunger: A Memoir of (My) Body*. A fiercely intelligent, honest and important writer, Gay's voice is an important feminist critique of the world we're living in.

some women being empowered
does not prove that the
patriarchy is dead.
It proves that some
of us are lucky

Roxane Gay
Quotation from Bad Feminists: Essays

76	4
Lw	
Lindy West	

LINDY WEST

Feminist commentator
USA; 1982–

Lindy West is shrill, loud and fat.

These are all words the American journalist and feminist commentator has used to describe herself.

Writing from the likes of the *New York Times* (who has described her writings as a decade of "national service"), the *Guardian* and *This American Life*, West has become an important feminist voice across a range of issues, in her efforts to reclaim women's autonomy over their own bodies, actions and words. She is a founder of I Believe You, It's Not Your Fault, an advice blog for teens, and she started #shoutyourabortion—a Twitter campaign to tackle shame and stigma. She speaks out on everything from sexual assault to the Trump administration. "Feminism," she has said, "is really just the long, slow realization that the things you love hate you." She has been a victim of heinous online trolling, highlighting the cost of being an outspoken woman online.

West is well-known for her writing on her body and leading the fat acceptance movement. In her book *Shrill: Notes from a Loud Woman*, she challenges the notions of shame and rejection that come from being fat in a world in which a woman's value is chiefly derived from whether or not she meets certain imposed physical ideals. She fights for fat people to, in her words, have "the permission to live."

West's refusal to adhere to conventional aesthetic demand is brave and necessary.

"The 'perfect body' is a lie. I believed in it for a long time, and I let it shape my life, and shrink it—my real life, populated by my real body. Don't let fiction tell you what to do."

Lindy West
(from *Shrill Notes from a Loud Woman*)

96 4
F
Femen

FEMEN

Eye-catching activists
Ukraine; founded 2008

A topless young woman in red shorts with long blonde hair stands in front of film cameras cutting down a 13-foot wooden cross with a chainsaw. This is FEMEN, the radical feminist group that campaigns against the patriarchy, religion and sex work. They protest and take direct action—always bare-chested. Since their formation, they've stormed Milan Fashion Week, Russia's St. Peter's Square, Davos and UEFA Euro 2012.

FEMEN was formed in Ukraine in 2008 by three friends, Anna Hutsol, Oksana Shachko and Alexandra Shevchenko, as a women's group with the intention of keeping the spirit of the country's recent Orange Revolution alive. Initially they were keen to protest against the sex tourism prevalent in Ukraine and took to the streets with price tags hanging off them.

A few years later, they staged their first topless protest—an act for which they would become internationally known. When they saw the furore it caused in the media, they decided that this was the most effective way of getting their message heard. The group believe that by displaying their semi-naked bodies they are reclaiming the female body, which has been owned, exploited, prostituted and commercialized by the patriarchy.

FEMEN organize training groups where they learn how to fight and resist arrest. The members of the group have received death threats, and they even allege abduction. In 2013, Tunisian Amina Tyler posted a bare-chested picture in solidarity on Facebook and a fatwa was issued for her to be punished with 100 lashes and stoned to death.

Some critics have expressed disappointment that women have to reveal their breasts in order to make a political statement, and the group has been accused of only having slim, "attractive" members. They have also been accused of being dismissive and patronizing toward Muslim women as they routinely protest against Islam.

In a time of "keyboard warriors," their direct action reflects an urgent and forceful face of feminism.

97   4
Pr
Pussy Riot

PUSSY RIOT

Modern-day punks
Russia; founded 2011

"Kill the Sexist," "Death to Prison, Freedom to Protests" and "Punk Prayer: Mother of God, Drive Putin Away"—these are songs by Pussy Riot, the fearless Russian political punk band.

Wearing signature colorful bandanas and performing punk rock protest songs on issues such as feminism, LGBT rights and Vladimir Putin, Pussy Riot, a group of around 11 young women, have proved themselves to be one of the most politically committed bands in the world.

In 2012, five members of the group performed in a Moscow cathedral to lambast the Church's support of Putin's dictatorial and homophobic leadership. Deemed sacrilegious, three of the members—Nadezhda Tolokonnikova, Maria Alyokhina, Yekaterina Samutsevich—were arrested.

The case gained international attention, with groups in the west including Amnesty International and FEMEN calling for their release. Celebrities such as Madonna and Björk offered support and, in 2012, Feminist Press released a collection of essays from the likes of Yoko Ono and post-punk singer Johanna Fateman in tribute. While Samutsevich was freed on probation, her bandmates spent 21 months in prison.

In recent years, Pussy Riot has continued to make protest music, including a song called "I Can't Breathe," referring to police brutality in America, and the anti-Trump song "Make America Great Again." The group has said they were inspired by the Riot Grrrl movement (page 138) of the 1990s.

101   4
Pl
Paris Lees

PARIS LEES

Transgender trailblazer
UK; 1989–

Transgender rights have come into the fore in recent years, becoming a key focus of Fourth Wave inclusionary feminism. Joe Biden, the former American Vice President, has called them the "civil rights issues of our times." Arguably, the Fourth Wave's demand for an intersectional approach to feminism has helped transgender men and women enter the mainstream, including Laverne Cox, Caitlyn Jenner and Munroe Bergdorf. In the UK, the number of children being referred to the Tavistock Clinic—a facility that aids children with transition—has rocketed, while newspaper columnists fill inches on the topic.

In the UK, Paris Lees has been a significant voice in pulling transgender rights out of the margins. She launched *META*, the first British magazine aimed at trans people, and was the first transgender TV presenter for BBC One and Channel 4, as well as the first openly transgender panellist on the UK's flagship late-night political program, *Newsnight*. She has also won several awards for her activism and advocacy.

Lees acknowledges it is still very difficult and even dangerous to be transgender. There are high suicide rates amongst young trans people, an increasing rate of transphobic crimes and widespread discrimination. In 2017 President Trump banned transgender people from serving in the military. As Lees said in 2013, "As anyone transgressing gender norms knows, you're constantly finding yourself in conflict with society, all the time—which is very, very tiring."

MARGOT FINK

Transgender activist
Australia; 1996–

Margot Fink is driving the fight for transgender rights in Australia.

Fink works with Minus18, the country's national organization for LGBTI youth, where she has shared her own experiences of transitioning. With support from the organization, Fink has placed particular focus on supporting the next generation. She led a campaign called Gender Is Not a Uniform to encourage schools to create safer spaces for gender-diverse students and she also devised All of Us, the first nationally approved teaching resource on LGBTI topics for Australian high schools. The

project consists of a series of videos sharing first-person experiences, including Fink's own, as well as lessons mapped to the
Australian curriculum. Fink designed the material with the aim of
making all students, regardless of gender or sexual orientation,
feel welcome. In 2016, she was a finalist for one of the country's
highest civic awards, Young Australian of the Year.

Fink's work is critical. Studies of the Australian transgender
community have found alarmingly high suicide rates. In 2015, a
17-year-old trans girl from Ohio, Leelah Alcorn, committed suicide,
leaving behind a Tumblr post in which she called for society to be
"fixed." By working with schools and the curriculum, Fink is pushing
the issue into the light—and igniting potentially life-saving conversations for the young people of Australia.

SISTERS UNCUT

Feminist activist group
UK; founded 2014

> We are Sisters Uncut. We stand united with all self-defining women,
> non-binary, agender and gender-variant people who live under the
> threat of domestic violence, and those who experience violence in
> their daily lives. We stand against the life-threatening cuts to domestic
> violence services. We stand against austerity.

This is the first paragraph from Sisters Uncut's "Feministo"
(a feminist manifesto). Sisters Uncut is a feminist activist group
working across the UK "taking direct action for domestic violence
services." And not only do they borrow the colors of the suffragettes, they borrow their famous adage "deeds not words."

Since their inception in 2014, born from the anti-austerity
movement of 2011, the group has staged a "dead in," lying on the
red carpet at the Leicester Square premiere of the film *Suffragette*, carrying signs that read "Dead Women Can't Vote." They
have stormed town halls with banners and smoke to protest
austerity measures that prohibit women's access to services.
Groups of campaigners have blocked bridges in London and in
Bristol to highlight the devastating effects of cutting off victims

from support. They have filled the Trafalgar Square fountains with red to mark the fact that two women are killed every week by their current or former partner.

The group demands legal aid, secure housing for women who cannot otherwise afford to leave, as well as the protection of refugee women, claiming "safety should not be subject to immigration status." As more specific groups continue to spring up across the UK to recognize the particular intersectional needs of different women, Sisters Uncut is a powerful, essential force holding government to account for the safety of women against male violence.

NIMCO ALI AND LEYLA HUSSEIN

Persistent activists
Somali and UK; 1982/83–, 1980–

One of the key conversations that has been born out of a renewed interest in gender equality is the issue of female genital mutilation, or FGM. Common in Africa, the Middle East and Asia, it also takes place in countries where it is illegal, such as the UK, where the National Society for Prevention of Cruelty to Children (NSPCC) suggests there are an estimated 137,000 women and girls who have been affected by it.

Much of our understanding of FGM is thanks to the tireless campaigning of survivors and that is no more true than in the case of Somali-born Nimco Ali and Leyla Hussein, who now reside in the UK and who founded the charity Daughters of Eve in 2010.

Through sharing their own experiences, they have worked hard to shatter many of the misunderstandings around FGM—chiefly, that it is not a cultural practice but a form of child abuse. Together they lobby the British government to protect the next generation of young girls and to make sure agencies, such as the police, education and health services, are aware of the condition and how to treat it. They appear on panels and debates to raise awareness, as well as supporting other victims. In 2016, Ali worked with the prime-time British BBC TV program *Call the Midwife* on a story line featuring FGM.

Progress is being made elsewhere, too: the issue has been addressed by world leaders such as David Cameron and Barack Obama, and studies are showing the cutting is starting to take place less frequently in African countries thanks to a global voice of resistance.

There's still a long way to go. FGM can leave women with a lifetime of health complications, including mental health issues such as anxiety and depression, and, in the UK, despite the fact that FGM was made illegal in 1985, there hasn't been a single prosecution.

Yet in less than a decade, Ali and Hussein have been a significant part of a force that has transformed a practice that was unknown and misunderstood, at best, into a pressing issue for today's government. Thanks to their honesty and persistence, the systematic abuse of girls in this way is being recognized and called out.

LENA DUNHAM

Controversial creative
USA; 1986–

Mentioning Lena Dunham in some corners of the internet can be explosive. The award-winning *Girls* creator, director, writer, executive producer and star has been accused of ignoring black women in her work and has had to make a string of public apologies for offensive comments she's made.

However, Dunham's feminist credentials shouldn't be completely overlooked. She loudly championed the idea of a female president in the run-up to the 2016 election, campaigning tirelessly to encourage young people to vote. Dunham's most effective feminism comes via her work around challenging traditional ideas of body image and how women are represented in the media.

While criticism of the lack of diversity in the TV series *Girls* is valid, Dunham did use her show to more realistically depict women's bodies (especially during sex), replacing the commonplace soft-porn aesthetic with something altogether more "flawed" and honest. In 2017, Dunham also appeared on the cover of American

Lena Dunham

Glamour, un-Photoshopped, in hot pants, with Dunham's cellulite center stage. It was a defiant statement in a society that still judges a woman by the size of her waist, where we are presented with "real" images by way of heavily filtered Instagram accounts, and with a celebrity culture low on diversity, big on one-note "perfection." By refusing to adhere to the impossible demands of today's skewed body culture, Dunham is heroically bursting one of today's most dangerous bubbles.

Dunham's work is highly personal (*Girls* is heavily autobiographical; she wrote a memoir and edits a newsletter called Lenny), but it is also political. Dunham continually uses her body and her platform to send a positive and reaffirming message of self-acceptance to women—and girls—around the world.

62   4
Lo
Lorella
Zanardo

LORELLA ZANARDO

Documentary filmmaker
Italy; 1957

In 2009, Lorella Zanardo, a former brand manager and marketing director from Milan, made a short documentary called *Il corpe delle donne*, or "Women's Bodies," intended to be shown in schools. Very quickly, however, it became a word-of-mouth sensation that the whole country was talking about.

The documentary explores the ways in which women are depicted on television, which, according to Zanardo, is overtly sexualized, often semi-naked, humiliating and represented as stupid, and older women who feel the need to endure high levels of plastic surgery, and that women's sole purpose is their relationship to men.

Not only did Zanardo's documentary hold a disturbing mirror up to sexism on Italian TV, *Il corpe delle donne* tells a bigger story about a deeply ingrained culture across Italian society. At the time, Silvio Berlusconi was simultaneously the country's prime minister, a media mogul and in charge of state television. This, of course, is the same Silvio Berlusconi who was accused of paying for sex with prostitutes and minors.

Zanardo's documentary identified how powerful institutions had reduced women to mere sex objects, and bombarded with these images on their TV screens daily, women were beginning to believe that this depiction of them was their true worth. Resurrecting a conversation that hadn't taken place since the 1970s, *Il corpe delle donne* was a brave indictment of a country steeped in sexism.

BEYONCÉ KNOWLES-CARTER

59   4

Bk

Beyoncé
Knowles-
Carter

Queen B
USA; 1981–

In 2013, Beyoncé Knowles clearly felt uneasy about the term "feminist." Speaking to British *Vogue* she said, "That word can be very extreme." "But I guess I am a modern-day feminist. I do believe in equality ... Why do you have to choose what type of woman you are? Why do you have to label yourself anything?"

Clearly, she'd changed her mind by the time she appeared at the VMAs in 2014. Alone on a stage, the singer stood in front of the word spelled out in 10-foot-high gold lights. Not only had Beyoncé accepted the label but her acceptance meant its arrival into the mainstream, too. (She wasn't the only high-profile pop star to change her mind. Taylor Swift and Katy Perry also embraced the word after initially rejecting it.)

Beyoncé's feminism became explicit with "Flawless" in 2013, when she sampled Chimamanda Ngozi Adichie's TED Talk, "We Should All Be Feminists," including the line "Feminist: the person who believes in the social, political, and economic equality of the sexes." Since then, Beyoncé has become increasingly political; at her 2016 Super Bowl performance, she paid homage to the Black Panthers and her video for "Formation" made references to police brutality. She campaigned for Hillary Clinton in 2016, and in 2017 she released a powerful video on International Day of the Girl, called *Freedom,* highlighting the oppression girls still face around the globe. On becoming a mother, she has also spoken of her endeavor to offer young black girls positive images of black women.

Black feminists, such as Adichie (page 180) and bell hooks (page 90), have been critical of Beyoncé's school of feminism—for

if a man can do it
a woman should be able to
too it's that simple

Beyoncé Knowles-Carter
Quotation from an interview in Elle in 2016

focusing on the needs of men in her songs, for upholding impossible beauty standards, and, most recently, for continuing the narrative of black women as victims. However, for many younger women, Beyoncé is a modern feminist who represents empowerment, black womanhood and ownership of her life and sexuality. To a whole generation, she embraces the kind of feminism born in the Third Wave that allows a woman to define her own feminist boundaries.

So great is the impact of Beyoncé on feminist discourse that higher-education institutions are offering academic courses on her.

EMMA WATSON

actress, feminist
UK; 1990

For millions of people, Emma Watson *is* Hermione Granger from Harry Potter, but in 2014, Watson adopted another role for which she would also become known: a feminist.

In that year, Watson became a UN Women's Goodwill Ambassador and gave a speech at the UN headquarters in New York where she launched her campaign, HeForShe.

She spoke of the sexism she had faced in her life, from being called bossy as a child to being sexualized by certain parts of the press as a young actress.

But mostly Watson used the speech to put an end to the "man-hating" connotations of feminism, and called for men to join the movement, arguing that everyone benefits from equality: "If men don't have to be aggressive in order to be accepted, women won't feel compelled to be submissive. If men don't have to control, women won't have to be controlled." In the 13-minute and 55-second speech Watson had launched herself as an exceptionally influential, powerful feminist voice. (Incredibly, she later revealed in an interview that she had been "encouraged" not to use the word "feminism" in the speech.)

In 2016, Watson launched another feminist campaign— Our Shared Shelf on Goodreads, a feminist book club that the world is invited to. Watson selects a book and readers can post their reviews online. Her selection tells the story of modern feminism—starting with Gloria Steinem's *On the Road* before moving on to, amongst others, Eve Ensler's *The Vagina Monologues*, Margaret Atwood's *The Handmaid's Tale*, Caitlin Moran's *How to Be a Woman*, Naomi Wolf's *The Beauty Myth* and bell hooks' *All About Love*. Watson has been known to hide copies of the books in public places around the world.

Watson is glamorous, smart and beautiful; she isn't angry or challenging or difficult and in that light she offers a fresh new face for Fourth Wave feminism, one that feels accessible, man-friendly and achievable. She's also proved she has a sense of humor—the perennial clichéd missing attribute of feminist women. When she was accused of showing too much skin in a *Vanity Fair* fashion shoot to be feminist, she brazenly said, "Feminism is about choice; I really don't know what my tits have to do with it."

CHIMAMANDA NGOZI ADICHIE

Writer, feminist
Nigeria; 1977–

Before Nigerian-born Chimamanda Ngozi Adichie was an internationally recognized feminist, she was a bestselling author. Most famously, her second novel, *Half of a Yellow Sun*, published in 2006, received the 2007 Orange Prize for Fiction and was made into a film. With creative-writing qualifications and fellowships from world-leading universities such as Princeton, Yale and Johns Hopkins, Adichie was regularly named as one of the world's most prominent young writers.

Fans of her novels and short stories might have already been aware of the feminist nature of her writing, but for many, her feminist agenda became most clear in her 2012 TED Talk, "We Should All Be Feminists." In the talk, which went on to be adapted into a book, Adichie describes life as a Nigerian woman, the double standards women and girls face and the oppressive nature of gender. She says, "The problem with gender is that it prescribes how we should be not how we are."

Adichie also addresses the word "feminism." And whilst she understands it is "so heavy with negative baggage; you hate men,

we   should all
be feminists

Chimamanda Ngozi Adichie
Quotation is Adichie's book title, published in 2014

you hate bras," Adichie embraces the word and defines it as, "A man or a woman who says, 'yes there's a problem with gender as it is today and we must fix it, we must do better.'" Her talk went viral.

In 2013, Beyoncé (page 177) sampled part of the talk on her single "Flawless" and her TED Talk sped round the world once more. After the whirlwind of press attention, Adichie said she was happy for young people to be talking about feminism, but she said of Beyoncé, "Still, her type of feminism is not mine, as it is the kind that, at the same time, gives quite a lot of space to the necessity of men. I think men are lovely, but I don't think that women should relate everything they do to men: did he hurt me, do I forgive him, did he put a ring on my finger?"

In 2017, Adichie published *Dear Ijeawele, or a Feminist Manifesto in Fifteen Suggestions.*

MALALA YOUSAFZAI

Brave activist
Pakistan; 1997

Malala needs little introduction. She has become an international symbol of resistance and bravery. Her name is synonymous with a selfless struggle to empower and educate girls. And Malala is still only 21 years old.

Malala Yousafzai was born in the Swat Valley region of Pakistan, where girls were banned from attending schools under Taliban rule. Her progressive father ran a chain of schools in the region and Malala looked to follow her father's example—believing that girls, too, should be educated. Her activism did not go unnoticed; in 2009, when she was 11, she wrote a blog for the BBC about her beliefs and efforts to bring education to the girls of the region. In 2010 the *New York Times* made a film about her. Her profile rose globally and as it did, she became a target for the Taliban.

In 2012 Yousafzai was shot in the head by a Taliban fighter. She recovered to full health in Birmingham, in the UK, where she moved for her safety.

Malala's bravery was celebrated around the globe. From 2012 to 2015, *Time* magazine featured her as one of the most

one child
one teacher
one book
one pen
can change
the world

Malala Yousafzai
Quotation from speech delivered at Nobel Peace Prize ceremony in 2014

influential people in the world. In 2014 she was the co-recipient of the Nobel Peace Prize, and at just 17, she became the youngest ever Nobel Laureate. Today Malala is a student at Oxford University and continues to advocate for education for girls via her own trust, The Malala Fund. Her work for the enfranchisement and right to education for all young people, especially girls, has made Malala one of the humanitarian heroes of our time.

Is she a feminist? Only after hearing Emma Watson's UN speech. Talking to Watson in 2015 she said, "I hesitated in saying am I a feminist or not and then after hearing your speech, when you said 'if not now, when? If not me, who?' I decided that there's no way and there's nothing wrong by calling yourself a feminist, so I am a feminist. And feminism is another word for equality."

AMANI AL-KHATAHTBEH

Muslim girl on a mission
USA; 1992–

Muslimgirl.net was the creation of a 17-year-old high-school student, started from her bedroom in 2009 with just $9 to pay for the domain name. The site has now over one million monthly unique users.

What started as a hobby has since become a full-time, fully invested mission to create a powerful voice that challenges stereotypes around Muslim women and girls. Fed up with the media's fearful and hateful depiction of Muslims in a post-9/11 world, today she and her volunteer staff are "taking back the narrative." She says, "We use our own voices to speak up for ourselves. We are raising the place of Muslim women in mainstream society. We are drawing awareness to the Qur'an's message of gender equality and Islam's principle of peace." And she is determined to dismantle the idea of Muslim women as "the Other." In an interview in 2016 she said, "Often we're just literally trying to show that we're human beings. And that's something that I feel we're at risk of being robbed of."

The content of the site ranges from the political: "Meet the Muslim pro-gun immigration lawyer running for senate," to the

we grew up
to become our
own saviors

Amani al-Khatahtbeh

practical: "This app makes it easy for Muslims to find room-mates," to the feminist: "Stop calling women selfish for choosing birth control," to fashion and beauty. Muslimgirl has even collab-orated with a beauty brand to create nail polish made from halal ingredients.

Muslim women face a barrage of imposed stereotypes forced upon them, from hateful discrimination to patronizing assump-tions. Al-Khatahtbeh is a tenacious young woman who has created a megaphone through which the next generation of Muslim women and girls can tell their own story.

TAWAKKOL KARMAN

Tireless journalist
Yemen; 1979–

At just 32, Yemeni Tawakkol Karman found herself in the eye of the Arab Spring. In a deeply conservative country, Karman was a revolutionary calling for the president of 32 years to stand down. Despite threats to her life and several arrests, Karman was a loud, influential voice for change in Yemen. For years, Karman led sit-ins and demonstrations in Tahrir Square, in the capital, Sana'a, and she followed the revolution as it spread across the Middle East. In 2011, she became the first Arab woman to win the Nobel Peace Prize for her "non-violent struggle for the safety of women and for women's rights to full participation in peacebuilding work."

A key concern of Karman's is women's rights. In 2005, she set up the Women Journalists Without Chains group, which seeks to promote education, culture and community development by focusing on women's and children's issues, as well as protecting a free media. During the Arab Spring she gave weekly lectures on women's rights.

Karman's efforts are valiant in a patriarchal country. The country ranked last in the World Economic Forum's 2016 Global Gender Gap report. Women still need a male guardian to approve a marriage and they don't have equal rights to men in divorce, child custody or inheritance.

After a brief period of positive momentum following the Arab Spring, war broke out between the new president and rebel groups. Yemen is now said to be suffering the largest humanitarian crisis in the world and Yemenis are reporting an increase in child marriage and domestic violence. In 2017 Karman said, "The world doesn't pay enough attention to Yemen. It's the forgotten land."

MARY AKRAMI

Risk-taking feminist
Afghanistan

Afghanistan is one of the most dangerous places in the world to be a woman due to high levels of illiteracy, high rates of child marriage, maternal mortality and domestic violence. In a country with a long history of conflict, which continues to face huge political and economic strife, not to mention its years of oppressive patriarchal Taliban rule, it would be easy to assume that women's rights have been forgotten. But the rights of Afghan women have not been forgotten by Mary Akrami.

Akrami is the founder and director of Afghan Women Skills Development Center, which set up the first known women's shelter for victims of domestic violence in the country in 2003. As well as accommodation, the center offers legal aid, health care and education.

In 2016, Akrami and her organization launched a restaurant called Boost in the capital, Kabul, which is fully staffed by women who have been through their shelter program, including victims of violence and vulnerable young women who have no support, family or income. In 2016, Akrami was selected as one of the BBC's 100 Women, a list of the most inspiring and influential women in the world.

Not only is Akrami offering a lifeline to women in a country that systematically works to oppress them, she told the BBC that she was keen to change perceptions of the women she works with: "These women are seen by society as victims, but I wanted to show that they aren't. They have power, they have capacity."

99   4
Lt
Li Tingting

LI TINGTING (AKA LI MAIZI)

Feminist fighter
China; 1989–

In China, it is dangerous to be a feminist. This is precisely what Li Tingting and four other young women, known as the Feminist Five, found out first-hand in 2015. The young women had planned to hand out stickers about sexual harassment on public transport for International Women's Day. Shortly after, coordinated raids took place on all their homes. The women were arrested and held in police detention for 37 days, where they suffered physical and psychological abuse.

Li Tingting and the other women are not easily deterred, however. After their release, Tingting recorded herself singing their defiant feminist anthem (to the tune of *Les Misérables'* "Do You Hear the People Sing?") and shared it on social media.

Growing up, Li Tingting witnessed her father beating her mother. Her experience as a woman and a lesbian in China has fuelled her determination to campaign on feminist issues. In 2012, Li Tingting and a few other women dressed as brides with blood smeared on their dresses to protest against domestic violence.

This sort of activism does not directly contravene Chinese law but is seen as increasingly provocative in light of the recent crackdown on any activism, along with heightened surveillance.

Li Tingting's feminism has been applauded and supported from across the world, from voices as powerful as Hillary Clinton. Today, Tingting gives talks in the UK and the U.S. in order to raise awareness of the feminist fight in China, something she believes is "going backward."

In light of the struggle of Tingting and the Feminist Five, cynicism in the west around the popularity of feminism needs to be countered with knowledge that in China women are risking their freedom for it.

79		4
	Lg	
Leymah Gbowee		

LEYMAH GBOWEE

Female leader
Liberia; 1972–

Leymah Gbowee is a woman who demanded peace. And after 14 years of brutal and devastating civil war, she achieved it.

Gbowee grew up witnessing war in Liberia, West Africa, and noticed how it particularly impacted upon women and children. As a young woman she trained to work with traumatized victims of rape and was politically active. She soon became involved in the peacebuilding movement.

By 2002, Gbowee was the recognized leader of the Women of Liberia Mass Action for Peace—recruiting local women of different ethnicities and different faiths at markets, churches and mosques to come together and pray and sing for peace. The women also threatened curses and to go on a sex strike—which inevitably caught the attention of the media.

All of Gbowee's efforts culminated in June 2003. Gbowee led a group of women to the peace negotiations in Accra, Ghana. Wearing all white, they picketed, protested and prayed. Eventually, Gbowee led the women inside the hotel where peace talks were taking place and the women linked arms, refusing to leave until peace had been made. In the following weeks, peace was officially declared.

In 2011, Gbowee, along with Liberian President Ellen Johnson Sirleaf and Yemeni activist Tawakkol Karman, was awarded the Nobel Peace Prize for her work for women's safety and her insistence that women would be part of the peace process.

Gbowee's fight for peace not only brought about the end of a war that saw the rape of children, starvation and disease, but proved that African women are effective and powerful peacebuilders.

"When women gather, great things will happen."

Leymah Gbowee

Male Allies

1. John Stuart Mill

An ally and inspiration to the British suffragettes, Mill called for women to be given the vote. In 1869, he published the essay *The Subjection of Women*, written with his wife, Harriet Taylor Mill, in which he argued the advance of all people was best for humankind.

2. Léon Richer

In the heart of the feminist movement of Paris in the late 1880s, Richer founded a feminist journal and also the French League for Women's Rights, alongside French suffragette leader Maria Deraismes.

3. Jeremy Bentham

The famous 18th-century English philosopher was a fierce advocate of gender equality and said it was at the root of his lifelong work as a reformist.

4. Qasim Amin

Considered one of the Arab world's first feminists, the Egyptian philosopher and jurist called for the liberation and education of women at the turn of the 20th century.

5. Frederick Douglass

"Right is of no sex, truth is of no color," the 18th-century abolitionist and suffragist said. Along with Elizabeth Cady Stanton and Susan B Anthony, the former slave founded the American Equal Rights Association in 1866.

6. John Stoltenberg

Radical feminist, scholar and author, Stoltenberg worked on projects to encourage men to not commit, and to prevent, sexual violence. He was married to Andrea Dworkin for 31 years.

7. Patrick Stewart

The famous British actor is an ambassador for Refuge, the domestic violence charity.

8. Barack Obama

A self-declared feminist, Obama signed the Lilly Ledbetter Fair Pay Act of 2009, his first bill signed into law.

9. Justin Trudeau

The Canadian PM loves to remind the world he's a feminist. He created a 50/50 cabinet, he encourages men to call out sexism and called for an investigation into missing and murdered indigenous women when he arrived in office.

10. Adam Jones

Leading Canadian scholar Adam Jones researches gender and international relations. In 2009 he published *Gender Inclusive: Essays on Violence, Men, and Feminist International Relations*.

Further Reading

Adichie, Chimamanda, *Dear Ijeawele, or a Feminist Manifesto in Fifteen Suggestions* (London: 4th Estate, 2017)

——, *Half of a Yellow Sun* (London: 4th Estate, 2016)

——, *We Should All Be Feminists* (London: 4th Estate, 2014)

Astell, Mary, *Serious Proposal to the Ladies: Parts I and II* (1694 and 1697. Repr. Peterborough, Canada: Broadview Press, 2002)

Atwood, Margaret, *The Handmaid's Tale* (London: Cape, 1985)

Bagge, Peter, *Woman Rebel: The Margaret Sanger Story* (Montreal: Drawn & Quarterly, 2013)

Bates, Laura, *Everyday Sexism* (London: Simon & Schuster, 2014)

——, *Girl Up* (London: Simon & Schuster, 2016)

Baumgardner, Jennifer, and Amy Richards, *Manifesta: Young Women, Feminism and the Future* (New York: Farrar, Straus & Giroux, 2000)

Beauvoir, Simone de, *The Second Sex* (1949. Repr. London: Penguin, 1972)

Bechdel, Alison, *Fun Home, A Family Tragicomic* (London: Cape, 2006)

Butler, Judith, *Bodies That Matter: On the Discursive Limits of Sex* (New York: Routledge, 1993)

——, *Gender Trouble: Feminism and the Subversion of Identity* (New York: Routledge, 1990)

Dworkin, Andrea, *Intercourse* (London: Martin Secker & Warburg, 1987)

——, *Pornography: Men Possessing Women* (London: Women's Press, 1981)

——, *Woman Hating* (New York: Penguin, 1974)

Ensler, Eve, *The Vagina Monologues* (London: Virago, 2001)

Firestone, Shulamith, *The Dialectic of Sex: The Case for Feminist Revolution* (New York: William Morrow, 1970)

Friedan, Betty, *The Feminine Mystique* (New York: W.W. Norton, 1963)

Fuller, Margaret, *Woman in the Nineteenth Century* (1845. Repr. New York: W.W. Norton, 1998)

Gay, Roxane, *Bad Feminist* (New York: Harper, 2014)

——, *Difficult Women* (New York: Grove Atlantic, 2017)

——, *Hunger: A Memoir of (My) Body* (New York: Harper, 2017)

Gouges, Olympe de, *Declaration of the Rights of Women* (1791. Repr. London: Ilex Press, 2018)

Greer, Germaine, *The Female Eunuch* (1970. Repr. London: Harper-Collins, 2006)

——, *The Whole Woman* (London: Doubleday, 1999)

hooks, bell, *Ain't I a Woman: Black Women and Feminism* (1981. Repr. London; Pluto Press, 1987)

——, *Feminism Is for Everybody* (London: Pluto Press, 2000)

——, *Feminist Theory: From Margin to Center* (1984. Repr. Abingdon: Routledge, 2014)

Irigaray, Luce, *Speculum of the Other Woman* (1975. Repr. Cornell: Cornell Univ Press, 1985)

——, *This Sex Which is Not One* (1977. Repr. Cornell: Cornell Univ Press, 1985)

Lorde, Audre, *A Burst of Light and Other Essays* (Mineola: Dover Publications, 1968)

Mill, John Stuart, *The Subjection of Woman* (1869. Repr. London: Hesperus Press, 2008)

Millett, Kate, *Sexual Politics* (1970. Repr. London: Virago, 1977)

Moran, Caitlin, *How to Be a Woman* (London: Ebury Press, 2011)

Rich, Adrienne, *Diving into the Wreck* (New York: W.W. Norton, 1974)

——, *Snapshots of a Daughter-in-Law* (New York: Harper & Row, 1963)

——, *Twenty-one Love Poems* (Michigan: Effie's Press, 1976)

Saadawi, Nawal El, *Memoir from the Woman's Prison* (Berkeley: Univ of California Press, 1994)

——, *Woman at Point Zero* (London: Zed Books, 1982)

Sandberg, Sheryl, *Lean In: Women, Work, and the Will to Lead* (London: W.H. Allen, 2015)

Solnit, Rebecca, *Men Explain Things to Me, and Other Essays* (London: Granta, 2014)

——, *The Mother of All Questions, Further Feminism* (London: Granta, 2017)

Steinhem, Gloria, *My Life on the Road* (New York: Random House, 2015)

Walker, Alice, *In Search of Our Mothers' Gardens* (San Diego: Harcourt Brace Jovanovich, 1983)

——, *The Color Purple* (San Diego: Harcourt Brace Jovanovich, 1982)

West, Lindy, *Shrill: Notes from a Loud Woman* (New York: Hachette Books, 2016)

Wolf, Naomi, *The Beauty Myth* (London: Chatto & Windus, 1990)

Woolstonecraft, Mary, *A Vindication of the Rights of Woman & of Men* (1790. Repr. Oxford: Oxford University Press 2008)

Index